DATA SCIENCE AND BIG DATA ANALYSIS

AS PER SPPU SYLLABUS

RAHUL M RAUT

Contents

Preface

Dear reader,

It gives us immense pleasure to write a new book on Data Science and Big Data Analysis. In this book we had tried to encapsulate all the concepts of the Data Science and Big Data Analysis. We tried to use easiest language so student can understand the concept in details.

We are thankful to all the people involved directly or indirectly in the making of this book. We are aslo Thankful to our parents parents and family member for theit patience and encouragement. We have jointly made every possible effort to eliminate all the errors inthis book.

This book not onlly cover the entire scope of the subject but explain the philosophy of the subject. This makes the understanding of this subject more clear and makes it more intresting.

Finally we wish all the readers of this book a very good luck.

## CHAPTER ONE

Introduction to Data science and Big Data

Data science combines multiple fields, including statistics, scientific methods, artificial intelligence (AI), and data analysis, to extract value from data. Those who practice data science are called data scientists, and they combine a range of skills to analyze data collected from the web, smartphones, customers, sensors, and other sources to derive actionable insights.

Data science encompasses preparing data for analysis, including cleansing, aggregating, and manipulating the data to perform advanced data analysis. Analytic applications and data scientists can then review the results to uncover patterns and enable business leaders to draw informed insights.

What is big data?

Big data is a combination of structured, semistructured and unstructured data collected by organizations that can be mined for information and used in machine learning projects, predictive modeling and other advanced analytics applications.

Systems that process and store big data have become a common component of data management architectures in organizations, combined with tools that support big data analytics uses Big Data can be defined as volumes of data available in varying degrees of complexity, generated at different velocities and varying degrees of ambiguity, that cannot be processed using traditional technologies, processing methods, algorithms, or any commercial off-the-shelf solutions.

Data defined as Big Data includes machine-generated data from sensor networks, nuclear plants, X-ray and scanning devices, and airplane engines, and consumer-driven data from social media. Big Data producers that exist within organizations include legal, sales, marketing, procurement, finance, and human resources departments.

Big Data example

Transportation

Big Data powers the GPS smartphone applications most of us depend on to get from place to place in the least amount of time. GPS data sources include satellite images and government agencies.

Airplanes generate enormous volumes of data, on the order of 1,000 gigabytes for transatlantic flights. Aviation analytics systems ingest all of this to analyze fuel efficiency, passenger and cargo weights, and weather conditions, with a view toward optimizing safety and energy consumption.

Big Data simplifies and streamlines transportation through:

- Congestion management and traffic control
  Thanks to Big Data analytics, Google Maps can now tell you the least traffic-prone route to any destination.
- Route planning
  Different itineraries can be compared in terms of user needs, fuel consumption, and other factors to plan for maximize efficiency.

- Traffic safety
Real-time processing and predictive analytics are used to pinpoint accident-prone areas.

Banking and Financial Services
The financial industry puts Big Data and analytics to highly productive use, for:

- **Fraud detection**
Banks monitor credit cardholders' purchasing patterns and other activity to flag atypical movements and anomalies that may signal fraudulent transactions.
- **Risk management**
Big Data analytics enable banks to monitor and report on operational processes, KPIs, and employee activities.
- **Customer relationship optimization**
Financial institutions analyze data from website usage and transactions to better understand how to convert prospects to customers and incentivize greater use of various financial products.
- **Personalized marketing**
Banks use Big Data to construct rich profiles of individual customer lifestyles, preferences, and goals, which are then utilized for micro-targeted marketing initiatives.

Big Data in Education Industry

- The education industry is flooded with huge amounts of data related to students, faculty, courses, results, and whatnot. Now, we have realized that proper study and analysis of this data can provide insights that can be used to improve the operational effectiveness and working of educational institutes.
  Following are some of the fields in the education industry that has been transformed by big data-motivated changes:
- **Customized and Dynamic Learning Programs:** Customized programs and schemes to benefit individual students can be created using the data collected based on each student's learning history. This improves the overall student results.
- **Reframing Course Material :** Reframing the course material according to the data that is collected based on what a student learns and to what extent by real-time monitoring of the components of a course is beneficial for the students.
- **Grading Systems :** New advancements in grading systems have been introduced as a result of a proper analysis of student data.
- **Career Prediction :** Appropriate analysis and study of every student's records will help understand each student's progress, strengths, weaknesses, interests, and more. It would also help in determining which career would be the most suitable for the student in the future.The applications of big data have provided a solution to one of the biggest pitfalls in the education system, that is, the one-size-fits-all fashion of academic set-up, by contributing to e-learning solutions.

Example
The University of Alabama has more than 38,000 students and an ocean of data. In the past when there were no real solutions to analyze that much data, some of them seemed useless. Now, administrators can use analytics and data visualization for this data to draw out patterns of students revolutionizing the university's operations, recruitment, and retention efforts.

Data explosion

What has led to this explosive growth of data? One answer is innovation. Innovation has transformed the way we engage in business, provide services, and the associated measurement of value and profitability. Three fundamental trends that shaped up the data world in the last few years are business model transformation, globalization, and personalization of services. Let us examine these in detail.

The definition of big data is data that contains greater variety, arriving in increasing volumes and with more velocity. This is also known as the three Vs.

The Five Vs of big data

- **Volume**

The amount of data matters. With big data, you'll have to process high volumes of low-density, unstructured data. This can be data of unknown value, such as Twitter data feeds, clickstreams on a web page or a mobile app, or sensor-enabled equipment. For some organizations, this might be tens of terabytes of data. For others, it may be hundreds of petabytes.

- **Velocity**

Velocity is the fast rate at which data is received and (perhaps) acted on. Normally, the highest velocity of data streams directly into memory versus being written to disk. Some internet-enabled smart products operate in real time or near real time and will require real-time evaluation and action.

- **Variety**

Variety refers to the many types of data that are available. Traditional data types were structured and fit neatly in a relational database. With the rise of big data, data comes in new unstructured data types. Unstructured and semistructured data types, such as text, audio, and video, require additional preprocessing to derive meaning and support metadata.

- **Veracity**

It refers to inconsistencies and uncertainty in data, that is data which is available can sometimes get messy and quality and accuracy are difficult to control.

Big Data is also variable because of the multitude of data dimensions resulting from multiple disparate data types and sources.

Example: Data in bulk could create confusion whereas less amount of data could convey half or Incomplete Information.

- **Value**

After having the 4 V's into account there comes one more V which stands for Value!. The bulk of Data having no Value is of no good to the company, unless you turn it into something useful.

Data in itself is of no use or importance but it needs to be converted into something valuable to extract Information. Hence, you can state that Value! is the most important V of all the 5V's.

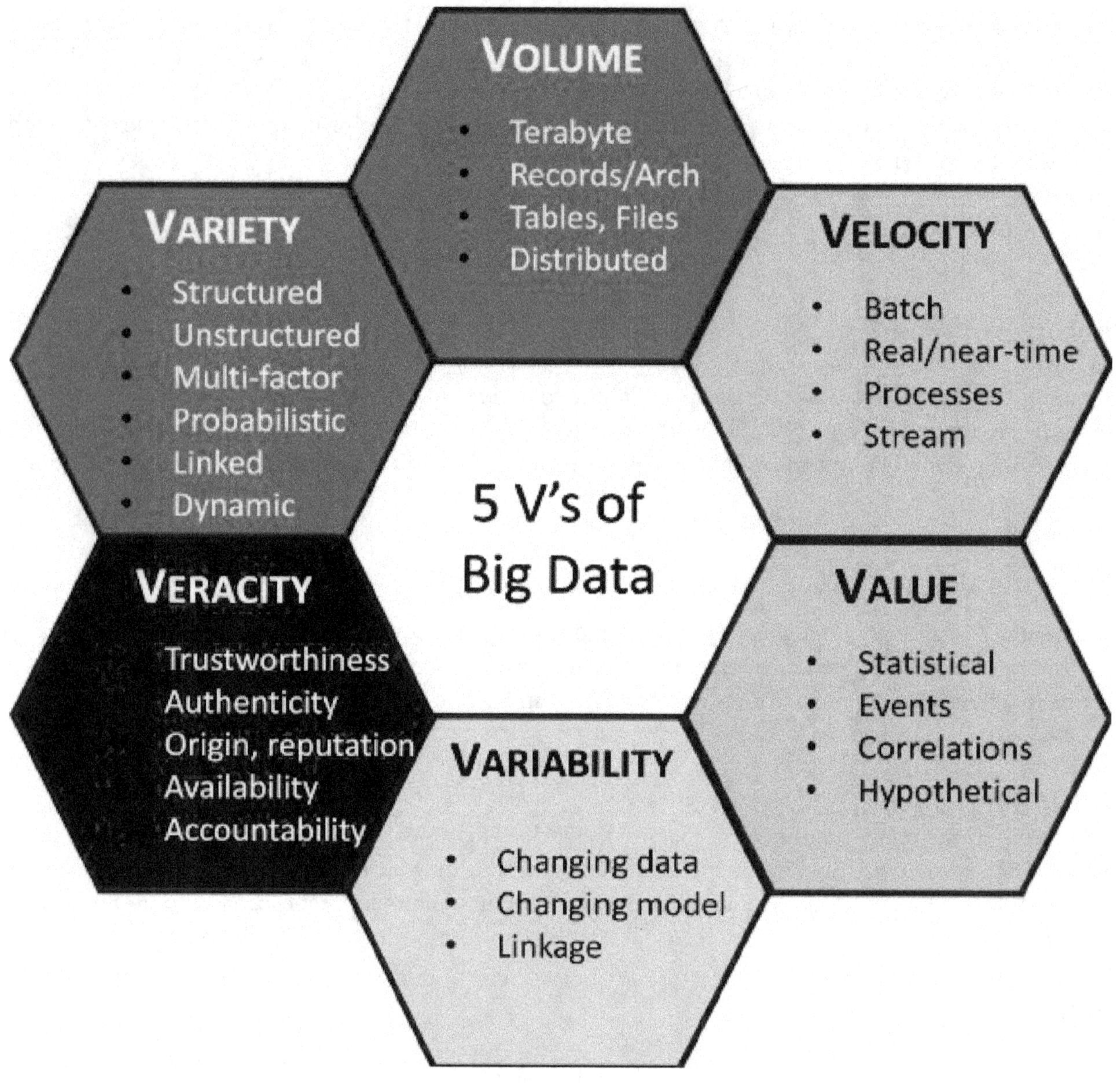

Fig. 5 V's of Big Data

- **Data volume**

Data volume is characterized by the amount of data that is generated continuously. Different data types come in different sizes. For example, a blog text is a few kilobytes; voice calls or video files are a few megabytes; sensor data, machine logs, and clickstream data can be in gigabytes. Traditionally, employees generated data. Today, for a given organization, customers, partners, competitors, and anyone else can generate data.

The following sections outline some examples of data generated by different sources.

Machine data

Application log

Clickstream logs

Emails

Contracts

Geographic information systems and geo-spatial data

- **Data velocity**

Velocity can be defined as the speed and direction of motion of an object. Constant velocity of an object is the motion of an object at constant speed and direction. With the advent of Big Data, understanding the velocity of data is extremely important. The basic reason for this arises from the fact that in the early days of data processing, we used to analyze data in batches, acquired over time. Typically, data is broken into fixed-size chunks and processed through different layers from source to targets, and the end result is stored in a data warehouse for further use in reporting and analysis. This data processing technique in batches or microbatches works great when the flow of input data is at a fixed rate and results are used for analysis with all process delays. The scalabilityand throughput of the data processing architecture is maintained due to the fixed size of the batches.

In the case of Big Data, the data streams in a continuous fashion and the result sets are useful

when the acquisition and processing delays are short. Here is where the need becomes critical for an ingestion and processing engine that can work at extremely scalable speeds on extremely volatile sizes of data in a relatively minimal amount of time. Let us look at some examples of data velocity.

Amazon, Facebook, Yahoo, and Google

The business models adopted by Amazon, Facebook, Yahoo, and Google, which became the de-facto business models for most web-based companies, operate on the fact that by tracking customer clicks and navigations on the website, you can deliver personalized browsing and shopping experiences. In this process of clickstreams there are millions of clicks gathered from users at every second, amounting to large volumes of data. This data can be processed, segmented, and modeled to study population behaviors based on time of day, geography, advertisement effectiveness, click behavior, and guided navigation response. The result sets of these models can be stored to create a better experience for the next set of clicks exhibiting similar behaviors. The sheer volume of data that is processed by these four companies has prompted them to open their technologies to the rest of the world. The velocity of data produced by user clicks on any website today is a prime example for Big Data velocity.

Sensor data

Another prime example of data velocity comes from a variety of sensors like GPS, tire-pressure

systems, On-Star-vehicle and passenger support services offered by General Motors, based on geospatial and location-based intelligence associated with the sensor on the automobile, heating and cooling systems on buildings, smart-meters, mobile devices, biometric systems, technical and scientific application, and airplane sensors and engines. The data generated from sensor networks can range from a few gigabytes per second to terabytes per second. For example, a flight from London to New York generates 650 TB of data from the airplane engine sensors. There is a lot of value in reading this information during the stream processing and postgathering for statistical modeling purposes.

Mobile networks

The most popular way to share pictures, music, and data today is via mobile devices. The sheer volume of data that is transmitted by mobile networks provides insights to the providers on the performance of their network, the amount of data processed at each tower, the time of day, the associated geographies, user demographics, location, latencies, and much more. The velocity of data movement is unpredictable, and sometimes can cause a network to crash. The data movement and its study have enabled mobile service providers to improve the QoS (quality of service), and associating this data with social media inputs has enabled insights into competitive intelligence.

Social media

Another Big Data favorite, different social media sites produce and provide data at different velocities and in multiple formats. While Twitter is fixed at 140 characters, Facebook, YouTube, or Flickr can have posts of varying sizes from the same user. Not only is the size of the post important, understanding how many times it is forwarded or shared and how much follow-on data it gathers is essential to process the entire data set. A post can go viral and have millions of posts and result in a huge volume to process, or a post may remain private yet generate additional data. The volatility of data generation is the data velocity problem experienced by social media

Big data Infrastructure and challenges

1. **Lack of knowledge Professionals**

To run these modern technologies and large Data tools, companies need skilled data professionals. These professionals will include data scientists, data analysts, and data engineers to work with the tools and make sense of giant data sets. One of the Big Data Challenges that any Company face is a drag of lack of massive Data professionals. This is often because data handling tools have evolved rapidly, but in most cases, the professionals haven't. Actionable steps got to be taken to bridge this gap.

Solution

Companies are investing extra money in the recruitment of skilled professionals. They even have to supply training programs to the prevailing staff to urge the foremost out of them. Another important step taken by organizations is purchasing knowledge analytics solutions powered by artificial intelligence/machine learning. These Big Data Tools are often traveled by professionals who aren't data science experts but have the basic knowledge. This step helps companies to save lots of tons of cash for recruitment.

2. **Lack of proper understanding of Massive Data**

Companies fail in their Big Data initiatives, all thanks to insufficient understanding. Employees might not know what data is, its storage, processing, importance, and sources. Data professionals may know what's happening, but others might not have a transparent picture. For example, if employees don't understand the importance of knowledge storage, they could not keep the backup of sensitive data. They could not use databases properly for storage. As a result, when this important data is required, it can't be retrieved easily.

Solution

Big Data workshops and seminars must be held at companies for everybody. Military training programs must be arranged for all the workers handling data regularly and are a neighborhood of large Data projects. All levels of the organization must inculcate a basic understanding of knowledge concepts.

3. **Data Growth Issues**

One of the foremost pressing challenges of massive Data is storing these huge sets of knowledge properly. the quantity of knowledge being stored in data centers and databases of companies is increasing rapidly. As these data sets grow exponentially with time, it gets challenging to handle. Most of the info is unstructured and comes from documents, videos, audio, text files, and other sources. This suggests that you cannot find them in the database.

Companies choose modern techniques to handle these large data sets, like compression, tiering, and deduplication. Compression is employed for reducing the number of bits within the data, thus reducing its overall size. Deduplication is the process of removing duplicate and unwanted data from a knowledge set. Data tiering allows companies to store data in several storage tiers. It ensures that the info is residing within the most appropriate space for storing. Data tiers are often public cloud, private cloud, and flash storage, counting on the info size and importance. Companies also are choosing Big Data tools, like Hadoop, NoSQL, and other technologies.

4. **Confusion while Big Data Tool selection**

Companies often get confused while selecting the simplest tool for giant Data analysis and storage. Is HBase or Cassandra the simplest technology for data storage? Is Hadoop, MapReduce ok, or will Spark be a far better option for data analytics and storage? These questions bother companies, and sometimes they're unable to seek out the answers. They find themselves making poor decisions and selecting inappropriate technology. As a result, money, time, efforts, and work hours are wasted.

Solution

You'll either hire experienced professionals who know far more about these tools. Differently is to travel for giant Data consulting. Here, consultants will provide a recommendation of the simplest tools supporting your company's scenario. Supporting their advice, you'll compute a technique then select the simplest tool for you.

5. Integrating Data from a Spread of Sources

Data in a corporation comes from various sources, like social media pages, ERP applications, customer logs, financial reports, e-mails, presentations, and reports created by employees. Combining all this data to organize reports may be a challenging task. This is a neighborhood often neglected by firms. Data integration is crucial for analysis, reporting, and business intelligence, so it's perfect.

Solution

Companies need to solve their Data Integration problems by purchasing the proper tools. A number of the simplest data integration tools are mentioned below:

6. Securing Data

Securing these huge sets of knowledge is one of the daunting challenges of massive Data. Often companies are so busy in understanding, storing, and analyzing their data sets that they push data security for later stages. This is often not a sensible move as unprotected data repositories can become breeding grounds for malicious hackers. Companies can lose up to $3.7 million for a stolen record or a knowledge breach.

Solution

Companies are recruiting more cybersecurity professionals to guard their data. Other steps taken for securing Big Data include: Data encryption Data segregation Identity and access control Implementation of endpoint security Real-time security monitoring Use Big Data security tools, like IBM Guardian.

Data Warehouse

Data Warehouse is a relational database management system (RDBMS) construct to meet the requirement of transaction processing systems. It can be loosely described as any centralized data repository which can be queried for business benefits. It is a database that stores information oriented to satisfy decision-making requests. It is a group of decision support technologies, targets to enabling the knowledge worker (executive, manager, and analyst) to make superior and higher decisions. So, Data Warehousing support architectures and tool for business executives to systematically organize, understand and use their information to make strategic decisions.

Data Warehouse environment contains an extraction, transportation, and loading (ETL) solution, an online analytical processing (OLAP) engine, customer analysis tools, and other applications that handle the process of gathering information and delivering it to business users.

A Data Warehouse (DW) is a relational database that is designed for query and analysis rather than transaction processing. It includes historical data derived from transaction data from single and multiple sources.

A Data Warehouse provides integrated, enterprise-wide, historical data and focuses on providing support for decision-makers for data modeling and analysis.

A Data Warehouse is a group of data specific to the entire organization, not only to a particular group of users.

It is not used for daily operations and transaction processing but used for making decisions.

A Data Warehouse can be viewed as a data system with the following attributes:

- ◦ It is a database designed for investigative tasks, using data from various applications.
- ◦ It supports a relatively small number of clients with relatively long interactions.
- ◦ It includes current and historical data to provide a historical perspective of information.
- ◦ Its usage is read-intensive.
- ◦ It contains a few large tables.

Three Tier Architecture:

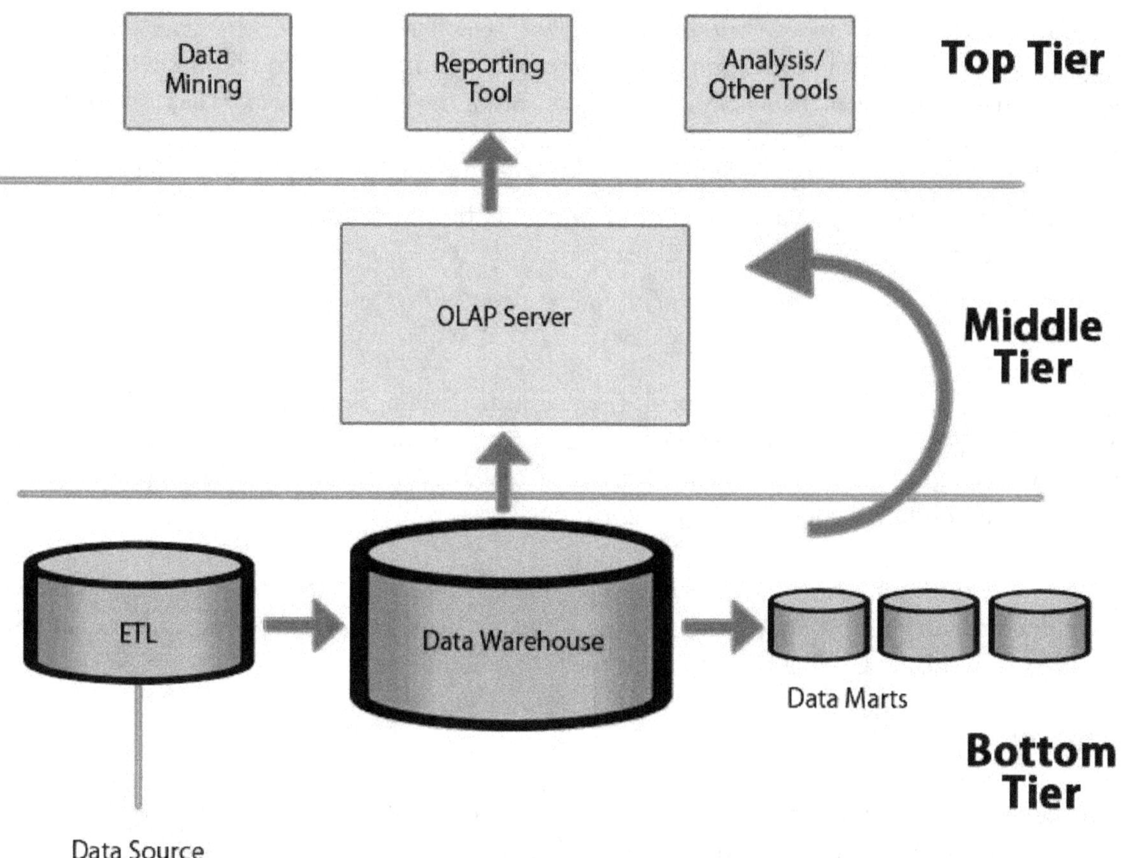

Fig. Data Warehouse Architecture

Bottom Tier (Data sources and data storage) :

1. The bottom Tier usually consists of Data Sources and Data Storage.
2. It is a warehouse database server. For Example RDBMS.
3. In Bottom Tier, using the application program interface(called gateways), data is extracted from operational and external sources.
4. Application Program Interface likes ODBC(Open Database Connection), OLE-DB(Open-Linking and Embedding for Database), JDBC(Java Database Connection) is supported.

Middle Tier :
The middle tier is an OLAP server that is typically implemented using either : A relational OLAP (ROLAP) model (i.e., an extended relational DBMS that maps operations from standard data to standard data); or A multidimensional

OLAP (MOLAP) model (ie, a special purpose server that directly implements multidimensional data and operations).

Top Tier :

The top tier is a front-end client layer, which includes query and reporting tools, analysis tools, and/or data mining tools (eg, trend analysis, prediction, etc.).

Shared Disk Architecture

Shared-disk architecture implements a concept of shared ownership of the entire database between RDBMS servers, each of which is running on a node of a distributed memory system.

Each RDBMS server can read, write, update, and delete information from the same shared database, which would need the system to implement a form of a distributed lock manager (DLM).

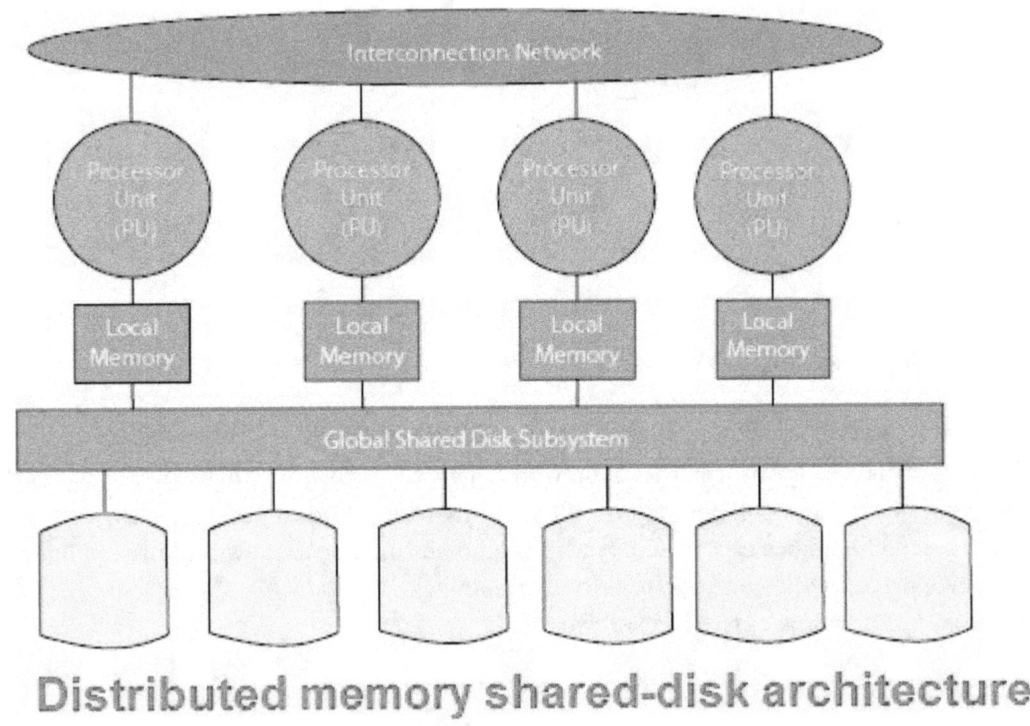

Fig. Shared Disk Architecture

Shared-Nothing Architecture

In a shared-nothing distributed memory environment, the data is partitioned across all disks, and the DBMS is "partitioned" across multiple co-servers, each of which resides on individual nodes of the parallel system and has an ownership of its disk and thus its database partition.

A shared-nothing RDBMS parallelizes the execution of a SQL query across multiple processing nodes. Each processor has its memory and disk and communicates with other processors by exchanging messages and data over the interconnection network. This architecture is optimized specifically for the MPP and cluster systems.

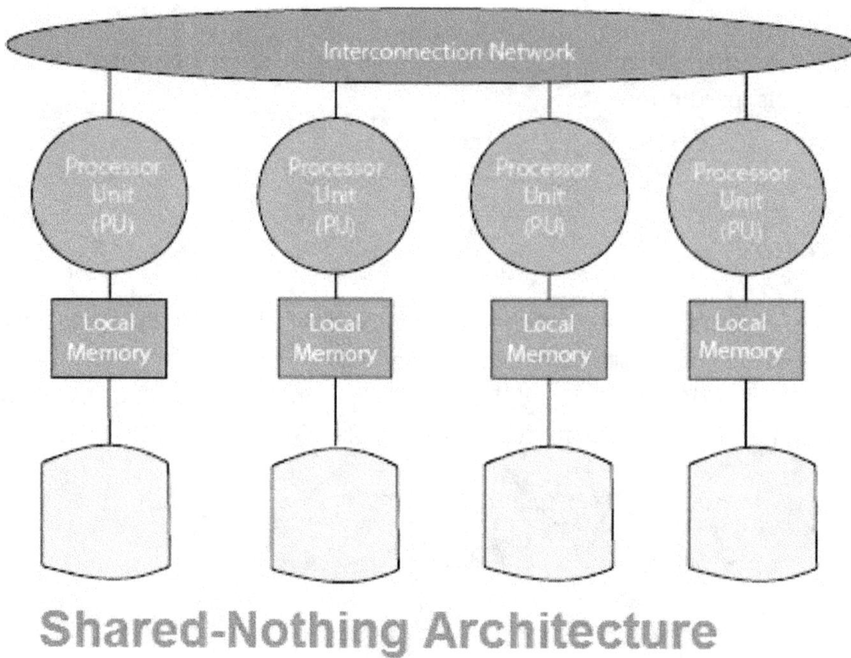

Fig. Shared Nothing Architecture

Reengineering the data warehouse

Replatforming

A very popular option is to replatform the data warehouse to a new platform including all hardware and infrastructure. There are several new technology options in this realm, and depending on the requirement of the organization, any of these technologies can be deployed. The choices include data warehouse appliances, commodity platforms, tiered storage, private cloud, and in-memory technologies.

There are benefits and disadvantages to this exercise.

Benefits:

- Replatforming provides an opportunity to move the data warehouse to a scalable and reliable platform.
- The underlying infrastructure and the associated application software layers can be architected to provide security, lower maintenance, and increase reliability.
- The replatform exercise will provide us an opportunity to optimize the application and database code.
- The replatform exercise will provide some additional opportunities to use new functionality.
- Replatforming also makes it possible to rearchitect things in a different/better way, which is almost impossible to do in an existing setup.

Disadvantages:

- Replatforming takes a long cycle time to complete, leading to disruption of business activities, especially in large enterprises and enterprises that have traditional business cycles b ased on
- waterfall techniques. One can argue that this can be planned and addressed to not cause any interruption to business, but this seldom happens in reality with all the possible planning.

- Replatforming often means reverse engineering complex business processes and rules that may be undocumented or custom developed in the current platform. These risks are often not considered during the decision-making phase to replatform.
- Replatforming may not be feasible for certain aspects of data processing or there may be complex calculations that need to be rewritten if they cannot be directly supported by the functionality of the new platform. This is especially true in cross-platform situations.
- Replatforming is not economical in environments that have large legacy platforms, as it consumes too many business process cycles to reverse engineer logic and documenting the same.
- Replatforming is not economical when you cannot convert from daily batch processing to microbatch cycles of processing.

Platform engineering

With advances in technology, there are several choices to enable platform engineering. This is fundamentally different from replatforming, where you can move the entire data warehouse. With a platform engineering approach, you can modify pieces and parts of the infrastructure and get great gains in scalability and performance.

The concept of platform engineering was prominent in the automotive industry where the focus was on improving quality, reducing costs, and delivering services and products to end users in a highly cost-efficient manner. By following these principles, the Japanese and Korean automakers have crafted a strategy to offer products at very competitive prices while managing the overall user experience and adhering to quality that meets performance expectations. Borrowing on the same principles, the underlying goal of platform engineering applied to the data warehouse can translate to:

- Reduce the cost of the data warehouse.
- Increase efficiencies of processing.
- Simplify the complexities in the acquisition, processing, and delivery of data.
- Reduce redundancies.
- Minimize customization.
- Isolate complexity into manageable modular environments.

Data engineering

Data engineering is a relatively new concept where the data structures are reengineered to create better performance. In this exercise, the data model developed as a part of the initial data warehouse is often scrubbed and new additions are made to the data model. Typical changes include:

- Partitioning—a table can be vertically partitioned depending on the usage of columns, thus reducing the span of I/O operations. This is a significant step that can be performed with minimal effect on the existing data, and needs a significant effort in ETL and reporting layers to refresh the changes. Another partition technique already used is horizontal partitioning where the table is partitioned by date or numeric ranges into smaller slices.
- Colocation—a table and all its associated tables can be colocated in the same storage region. This is a simple exercise but provides powerful performance benefits.
- Distribution—a large table can be broken into a distributed set of smaller tables and used. The downside is when a user asks for all the data from the table, we have to join all the underlying tables.
- New data types—several new data types like geospatial and temporal data can be used in the data architecture and current workarounds for such data can be retired. This will provide a significant performance boost.
- New database functions—several new databases provid native functions like scalar tables and indexed views, and can be utilized to create performance boosts. Though there are several possibilities, data engineering can be done only if all other possibilities have been exhausted.

The reason for this is there is significant work that needs to be done in the ETL and reporting layers if the data layer has changes. This requires more time and increases risk and cost. Therefore, data engineering is not often a preferred technique when considering reengineering or modernizing the data warehouse.

Big Data Learning approach

important as many organizations both public and private have been collecting massive amounts of domain-specific information, which can contain useful information about problems such as national intelligence, cyber security, fraud detection, marketing, and medical informatics. Companies such as Google and Microsoft are analysing large volumes of data for business analysis and decisions, impacting existing and future technology. Deep Learning algorithms extract high-level, complex abstractions as data representations through a hierarchical learning process. Complex abstractions are learnt at a given level based on relatively simpler abstractions formulated in the preceding level in the hierarchy. A key benefit of Deep Learning is the analysis and learning of massive amounts of unsupervised data, making it a valuable tool for Big Data Analytics where raw data is largely unlabelled and un-categorized

Machine learning algorithms are useful for collecting, analysing and integrating data for large organizations. They can be implemented in all elements of big data operations including data labelling and segmentation, data analytics and scenario simulations.

There are three types of machine learning methods

1. Supervised Learning

As its name suggests, Supervised machine learning is based on supervision. It means in the supervised learning technique, we train the machines using the "labelled" dataset, and based on the training, the machine predicts the output. Here, the labelled data specifies that some of the inputs are already mapped to the output. More preciously, we can say; first, we train the machine with the input and corresponding output, and then we ask the machine to predict the output using the test dataset.

1. Unsupervised Learning

Unsupervised learning is different from the Supervised learning technique; as its name suggests, there is no need for supervision. It means, in unsupervised machine learning, the machine is trained using the unlabelled dataset, and the machine predicts the output without any supervision.

In unsupervised learning, the models are trained with the data that is neither classified nor labelled, and the model acts on that data without any supervision.

The main aim of the unsupervised learning algorithm is to group or categories the unsorted dataset according to the similarities, patterns, and differences. Machines are instructed to find the hidden patterns from the input dataset.

3. Reinforcement Learning

Reinforcement learning works on a feedback-based process, in which an AI agent (A software component) automatically explore its surrounding by hitting & trail, taking action, learning from experiences, and improving its performance. Agent gets rewarded for each good action and get punished for each bad action; hence the goal of reinforcement learning agent is to maximize the rewards.

In reinforcement learning, there is no labelled data like supervised learning, and agents learn from their experiences only.

The Reinforcement learning process is similar to a human being; for example, a child learns various things by experiences in his day-to-day life. An example of reinforcement learning is to play a game, where the Game is the environment, moves of an agent at each step define states, and the goal of the agent is to get a high score. Agent receives feedback in terms of punishment and rewards

Relationship between Artificial Intelligence, Machine Learning and Data Science

Artificial Intelligence:

Artificial intelligence is a field of computer science where the computer systems are developed such that it can perform tasks which can be done by human intelligence. There are variety of tasks such as speech recognition, image recognition, decision making systems etc. The term artificial intelligence itself is self-explanatory. This intelligence in computers systems are built by humans using some techniques and algorithms like Natural Language Processing (NLP) or computer vision etc. The machines are developed with the intent of making it intelligent enough to work and react like humans. Data plays an important part of AI. It is with the help of the large amount of data known as big data that these systems perform well. The field of artificial intelligence is vast and it comprises of subfields like machine learning and deep learning.

Machine learning:

Machine learning is a subfield of artificial intelligence. Machine learning is used to make future predictions for a particular problem based on the historical data. The most common example of application of machine learning that you can relate to, is detecting whether an email is spam or not. You may have noticed that your email provider helps to detect the spam emails based on the previous email that you marked as spam. This prediction is done using various algorithms like regression or classification. To build such algorithms you need huge amount of data. The larger the data better the predictions. Machine learning has a subfield known as deep learning which is inspired from the way our human brain is wired. It contains multiple layer of neural networks. This network can be built in a complex way which helps in predicting better results. Just like our brains, the neural network also contains neurons which are interconnected with each other. There is an input layer, an output layer and it can also contain one or more hidden layers. The following diagram shows a simple representation of neural network.

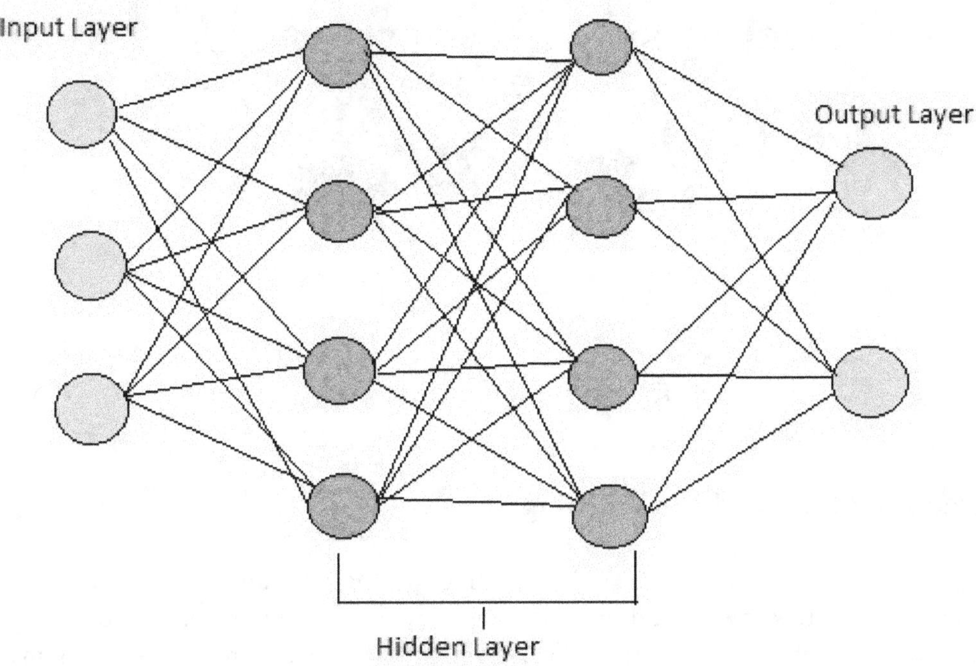

Fig. Neural Network Architecture

Data Science:

Data science is a field where data scientist derives valuable insights from large volumes of data. The insights derived by data scientists helps companies grow their business. Data science involves analysis of data, modelling of data etc. This field involves part of machine learning for making predictions and for modelling. The other sections of data science include data extraction, data exploration, data preparation, data visualisation etc. This field is growing rapidly as the amount of data being generated day by day is growing exponentially. This generated data needs to be processed and used to grow business. The data scientists are people who have good expertise in programming, machine learning, domain knowledge, mathematics and statistics. A Data Scientist is also known as a person who is better at statistics than any software engineer and better at software engineering than any statistician.

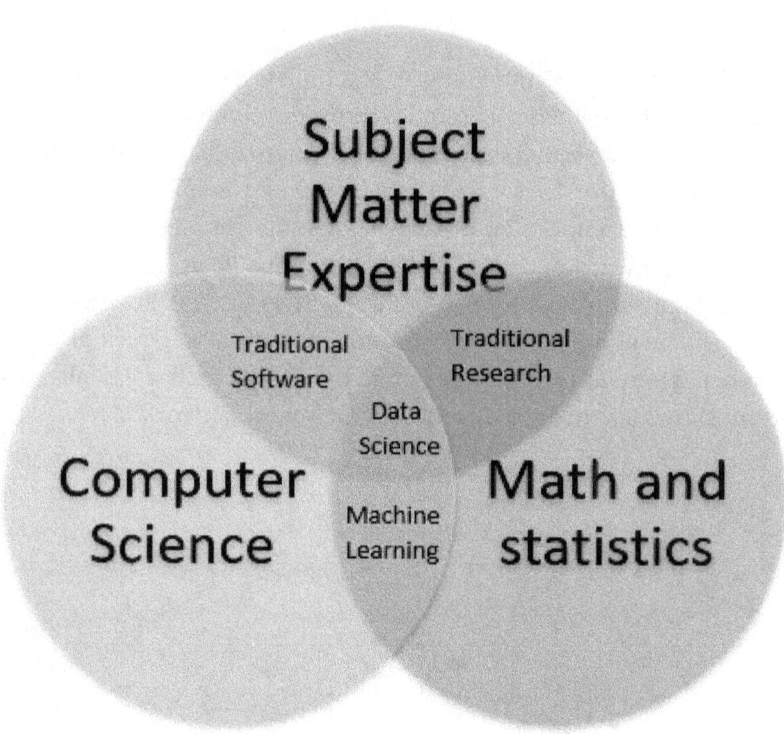

Fig. Overview of Data Science

Difference Between Big Data and Data Mining

Big Data: It is huge, large or voluminous data, information or the relevant statistics acquired by the large organizations and ventures. Many software and data storage created and prepared as it is difficult to compute the big data manually. It is used to discover patterns and trends and make decisions related to human behavior and interaction technology.

- The goal is to make data more vital and usable i.e. by extracting only important information from the huge data within existing traditional aspects.
- It is only automated as computing huge data is difficult.
- It focuses and works with all form of data i.e. structured, unstructured or semi-structured.
- It is mainly used for business purposes and customer satisfaction. Big Data is a mine.
- It is a super set of Data Mining.
- It is more involved with the processes of handling voluminous data. Data can only be large.

Data Mining: Data Mining is a technique to extract important and vital information and knowledge from a huge set/libraries of data. It derives insight by carefully extracting, reviewing, and processing the huge data to find out pattern and co-relations which can be important for the business. It is analogous to the gold mining where golds are extracted from rocks and sands.

- The goal is same as Big Data as it is one of the tool of Big Data.
- It is manual as well as automated in nature.
- It only focuses on only one form of data. i.e. structured.
- It is used to create certain business insights. Data mining is a manager of the mine.
- It is a sub set of Big Data. i.e. one of the tools.
- It is a tool to dig up the vital information from the large data. Data can be large as well as small.

Data Science life Cycle:

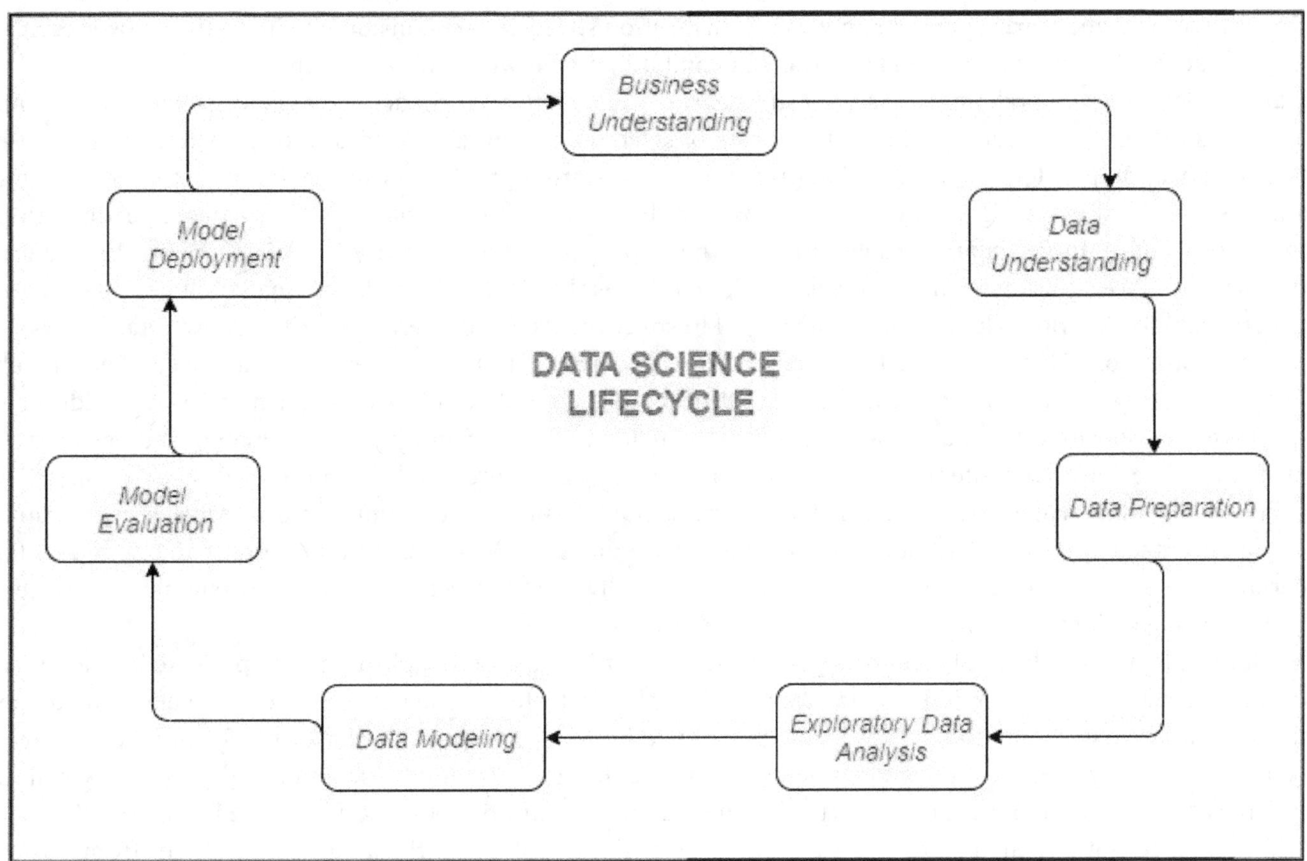

Fig. Data Science Life cycle

1. **Business Understanding:** The complete cycle revolves around the enterprise goal. What will you resolve if you do no longer have a specific problem? It is extraordinarily essential to apprehend the commercial enterprise goal sincerely due to the fact that will be your ultimate aim of the analysis. After desirable perception only we can set the precise aim of evaluation that is in sync with the enterprise objective. You need to understand if the customer desires to minimize savings loss, or if they prefer to predict the rate of a commodity, etc.

2. **Data Understanding:** After enterprise understanding, the subsequent step is data understanding. This includes a series of all the reachable data. Here you need to intently work with the commercial enterprise group as they are certainly conscious of what information is present, what facts should be used for this commercial enterprise problem, and different information. This step includes describing the data, their structure, their relevance, their records type. Explore the information using graphical plots. Basically, extracting any data that you can get about the information through simply exploring the data.

3. **Preparation of Data:** Next comes the data preparation stage. This consists of steps like choosing the applicable data, integrating the data by means of merging the data sets, cleaning it, treating the lacking values through either eliminating them or imputing them, treating inaccurate data through eliminating them, additionally test for outliers the use of box plots and cope with them. Constructing new data, derive new elements from present ones. Format the data into the preferred structure, eliminate undesirable columns and features. Data preparation is the most time-consuming but arguably the most essential step in the complete existence cycle. Your model will be as accurate as your data.

4. **Exploratory Data Analysis:** This step includes getting some concept about the answer and elements affecting it, earlier than constructing the real model. Distribution of data inside distinctive variables of a character is explored graphically the usage of bar-graphs, Relations between distinct aspects are captured via graphical representations like scatter plots and warmth maps. Many data visualization strategies are considerably used to discover each and every characteristic individually and by means of combining them with different features.

5. **Data Modeling:** Data modeling is the coronary heart of data analysis. A model takes the organized data as input and gives the preferred output. This step consists of selecting the suitable kind of model, whether the problem is a classification problem, or a regression problem or a clustering problem. After deciding on the model family, amongst the number of algorithms amongst that family, we need to cautiously pick out the algorithms to put into effect and enforce them. We need to tune the hyperparameters of every model to obtain the preferred performance. We additionally need to make positive there is the right stability between overall performance and generalizability. We do no longer desire the model to study the data and operate poorly on new data.

6. **Model Evaluation:** Here the model is evaluated for checking if it is geared up to be deployed. The model is examined on an unseen data, evaluated on a cautiously thought out set of assessment metrics. We additionally need to make positive that the model conforms to reality. If we do not acquire a quality end result in the evaluation, we have to re-iterate the complete modelling procedure until the preferred stage of metrics is achieved. Any data science solution, a machine learning model, simply like a human, must evolve, must be capable to enhance itself with new data, adapt to a new evaluation metric. We can construct more than one model for a certain phenomenon, however, a lot of them may additionally be imperfect. The model assessment helps us select and construct an ideal model.

7. **Model Deployment:** The model after a rigorous assessment is at the end deployed in the preferred structure and channel. This is the last step in the data science life cycle. Each step in the data science life cycle defined above must be laboured upon carefully. If any step is performed improperly, and hence, have an effect on the subsequent step and the complete effort goes to waste. For example, if data is no longer accumulated properly, you'll lose records and you will no longer be constructing an ideal model. If information is not cleaned properly, the model will no longer work. If the model is not evaluated properly, it will fail in the actual world. Right from Business perception to model deployment, every step has to be given appropriate attention, time, and effort.

## CHAPTER TWO

Mathematical Foundation of Big Data

Probability

probability theory, a branch of mathematics concerned with the analysis of random phenomena. The outcome of a random event cannot be determined before it occurs, but it may be any one of several possible outcomes. The actual outcome is considered to be determined by chance.

The word probability has several meanings in ordinary conversation. Two of these are particularly important for the development and applications of the mathematical theory of probability. One is the interpretation of probabilities as relative frequencies, for which simple games involving coins, cards, dice, and roulette wheels provide examples. The distinctive feature of games of chance is that the outcome of a given trial cannot be predicted with certainty, although the collective results of a large number of trials display some regularity. For example, the statement that the probability of "heads" in tossing a coin equals one-half, according to the relative frequency interpretation, implies that in a large number of tosses the relative frequency with which "heads" actually occurs will be approximately one-half, although it contains no implication concerning the outcome of any given toss. There are many similar examples involving groups of people, molecules of a gas, genes, and so on.

Random Variables:

In probability, a real-valued function, defined over the sample space of a random experiment, is called a random variable. That is, the values of the random variable correspond to the outcomes of the random experiment. Random variables could be either discrete or continuous.

A random variable is a numerical description of the outcome of a statistical experiment. A random variable that may assume only a finite number or an infinite sequence of values is said to be discrete; one that may assume any value in some interval on the real number line is said to be continuous. For instance, a random variable representing the number of automobiles sold at a particular dealership on one day would be discrete, while a random variable representing the weight of a person in kilograms (or pounds) would be continuous.

Types of Random Variable

As discussed in the introduction, there are two random variables, such as:

- Discrete Random Variable
- Continuous Random Variable

Let's understand these types of variables in detail along with suitable examples below.

Discrete Random Variable

A discrete random variable can take only a finite number of distinct values such as 0, 1, 2, 3, 4, ... and so on. The probability distribution of a random variable has a list of probabilities compared with each of its possible values known as probability mass function.

In an analysis, let a person be chosen at random, and the person's height is demonstrated by a random variable. Logically the random variable is described as a function which relates the person to the person's height. Now in relation with the random variable, it is a probability distribution that enables the calculation of the probability that the height is in any subset of likely values, such as the likelihood that the height is between 175 and 185 cm, or the possibility that the height is either less than 145 or more than 180 cm. Now another random variable could be the person's age which could be either between 45 years to 50 years or less than 40 or more than 50.

Continuous Random Variable

A numerically valued variable is said to be continuous if, in any unit of measurement, whenever it can take on the values a and b. If the random variable X can assume an infinite and uncountable set of values, it is said to be a continuous random variable. When X takes any value in a given interval (a, b), it is said to be a continuous random variable in that interval.

Formally, a continuous random variable is such whose cumulative distribution function is constant throughout. There are no "gaps" in between which would compare to numbers which have a limited probability of occurring. Alternately, these variables almost never take an accurately prescribed value c but there is a positive probability that its value will rest in particular intervals which can be very small.

A typical example of a random variable is the outcome of a coin toss. Consider a probability distribution in which the outcomes of a random event are not equally likely to happen. If random variable, Y, is the number of heads we get from tossing two coins, then Y could be 0, 1, or 2. This means that we could have no heads, one head, or both heads on a two-coin toss.

However, the two coins land in four different ways: TT, HT, TH, and HH. Therefore, the $P(Y=0) = 1/4$ since we have one chance of getting no heads (i.e., two tails [TT] when the coins are tossed). Similarly, the probability of getting two heads (HH) is also 1/4. Notice that getting one head has a likelihood of occurring twice: in HT and TH. In this case, $P(Y=1) = 2/4 = 1/2$.

Sample Space and Event

The fundamental ingredient of probability theory is an experiment that can be repeated, at least hypothetically, under essentially identical conditions and that may lead to different outcomes on different trials.

The set of all possible outcomes of an experiment is called a "sample space." The experiment of tossing a coin once results in a sample space with two possible outcomes, "heads" and "tails." Tossing two dice has a sample space with 36 possible outcomes, each of which can be identified with an ordered pair (i, j), where i and j assume one of the values 1, 2, 3, 4, 5, 6 and denote the faces showing on the individual dice. It is important to think of the dice as identifiable (say by a difference in colour), so that the outcome (1, 2) is different from (2, 1).

An "event" is a well-defined subset of the sample space. For example, the event "the sum of the faces showing on the two dice equals six" consists of the five outcomes (1, 5), (2, 4), (3, 3), (4, 2), and (5, 1).

Simple Events

Any event consisting of a single point of the sample space is known as a **simple event** in probability. For example, if S = {56 , 78 , 96 , 54 , 89} and E = {78} then E is a simple event.

Compound Events

Contrary to the simple event, if any event consists of more than one single point of the sample space then such an event is called a **compound event**. Considering the same example again, if S = {56 ,78 ,96 ,54 ,89}, E_1 = {56 ,54 }, E_2 = {78 ,56 ,89 } then, E_1 and E_2 represent two compound events.

Algebra of Events

S such that A ⊆ S, B ⊆ S and C ⊆ S that means <u>subsets</u> of S. Let's define the algebra of these events one by one.

Complementary Event

For every event A, there corresponds another event A′ called the complementary event to A. It is also called the event 'not A'.

A′ = {ω : ω ∈ S and ω ∉ A} = S − A

Here, A is the event, ω is the outcome associated with the event A and S is the sample space.

We can show the complementary event using venn diagram as:

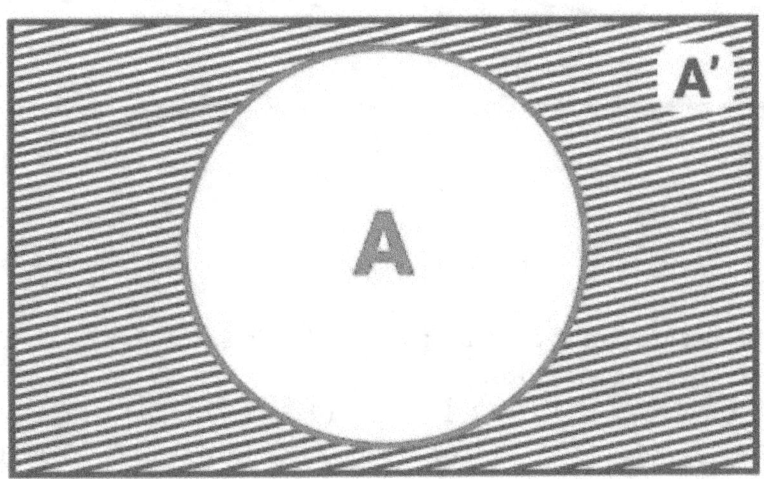

Fig. Venn Diagram for complementry event

For example, consider the experiment of 'tossing three coins'. The associated sample space can be written as:

S = {HHH, HHT, HTH, THH, HTT, THT, TTH, TTT}

Let A be the event of getting 'at least two heads'.

Thus, the outcomes associated with the event A = {HHT, HTH, THH, HHH}

From this, we can say that, for the outcome HTT the event A has not occurred. In other words, we may say that the event 'not A' has occurred. Therefore, the complementary event 'not A' of the event A is A′.

A′ = {THH, HTT, THT, TTH, TTT}

The Event 'A or B'

The Event '**A or B**' is the union of two sets A and B, denoted by **A ∪ B** containing all those elements in A or B or both. When sets A and B are two events associated with a sample space, then A ∪ B is either A or B or both. This event 'A ∪ B' is also called 'A or B'.

Therefore Event 'A or B' = A ∪ B = {ω: ω ∈ A or ω ∈ B}

The venn diagram representation of A or B, i.e. A ∪ B is given below:

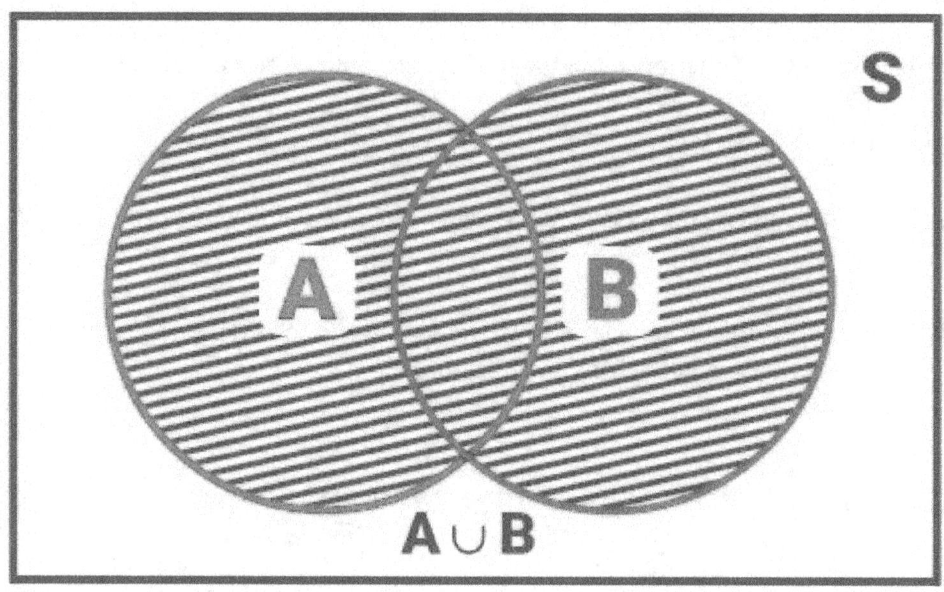

Fig. Venn diagram for A ∪ B

For example, consider the experiment of throwing two dice at a time.

The associated sample space can be written as:

S = {(1, 1), (1, 2), (1, 3), (1, 4), (1, 5), (1, 6), (2, 1), (2, 2), (2, 3), (2, 4), (2, 5), (2, 6), (3, 1), (3, 2), (3, 3), (3, 4), (3, 5), (3, 6), (4, 1), (4, 2), (4, 3), (4, 4), (4, 5), (4, 6), (5, 1), (5, 2), (5, 3), (5, 4), (5, 5), (5, 6), (6,1), (6, 2), (6, 3), (6, 4), (6, 5), (6, 6)}

Let A be the event of getting a sum of two scores will be a multiple of 3 and B be the event of getting same scores on both dice.

The outcomes associated with these events are:

A = {(1, 2), (2, 1), (1, 5), (5, 1), (2, 4), (4, 2), (3, 3), (3, 6), (6, 3), (4, 5), (5, 4), (6, 6)}

B = {(1, 1), (2, 2), (3, 3), (4, 4), (5, 5), (6, 6)}

Therefore, A ∪ B = {(1, 1), (1, 2), (1, 5), (2, 1), (2, 2), (2, 4), (3, 3), (3, 6), (4, 2), (4, 4), (4, 5), (5, 1), (5,4), (5, 5), (6, 3), (6, 6)}

The Event 'A and B'

The Event 'A and B' is the intersection of two sets A ∩ B is the set of those common elements to both A and B, i.e., the elements belong to both 'A and B'.

If A and B are two events, then the set A ∩ B denotes the event 'A and B'. It is expressed as:

A ∩ B = {ω: ω ∈ A and ω ∈ B}

Below figure shows the set A ∩ B using Venn diagram.

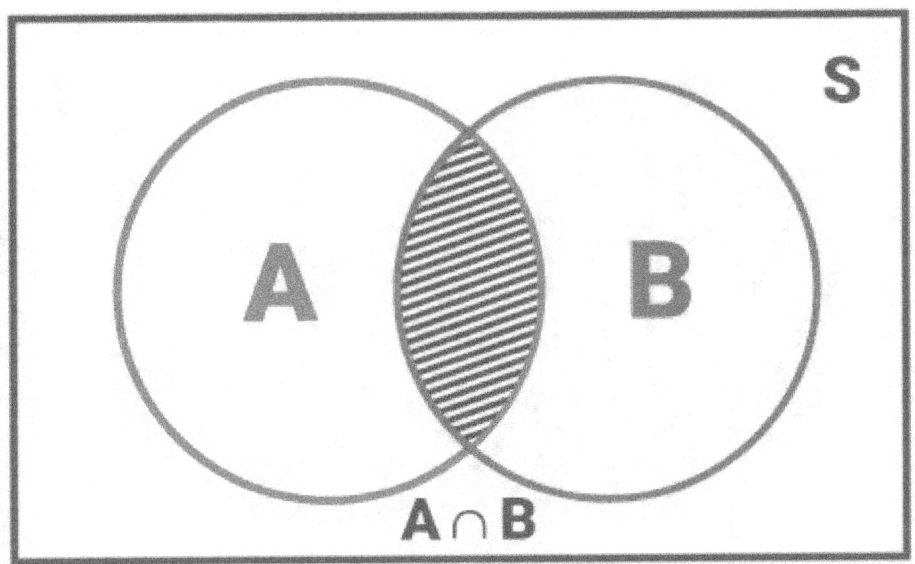

Fig. Venn diagramm for A ∩ B

Again, consider the experiment of throwing two dice at a time.

The associated sample space can be written as:

S = {(1, 1), (1, 2), (1, 3), (1, 4), (1, 5), (1, 6), (2, 1), (2, 2), (2, 3), (2, 4), (2, 5), (2, 6), (3, 1), (3, 2), (3, 3), (3, 4), (3, 5), (3, 6), (4, 1), (4, 2), (4, 3), (4, 4), (4, 5), (4, 6), (5, 1), (5, 2), (5, 3), (5, 4), (5, 5), (5, 6), (6,1), (6, 2), (6, 3), (6, 4), (6, 5), (6, 6)}

Let A be the event of getting a score on the second die is 5 and B be the event of getting sum of scores on dice is 10 & more than 10.

The outcomes associated with these events are:

A = {(1, 5), (2, 5), (3, 5), (4, 5), (5, 5), (6, 5)}

B = {(3, 6), (6, 4), (5, 5), (5, 6), (6, 5), (6, 6)}

Therefore, A ∩ B = {(5, 5), (6, 5)}

The Event 'A but not B'

The event **A but not B** is the set **A − B**, i.e. difference of sets A and B. It is the set of all those elements which are in A but not in B. We can calculate the set A − B using the expression:

A − B = A ∩ B′

Thus, A − B = {ω: ω ∈ A and ω ∉ B}

The below figure helps in understanding the event A but not B.

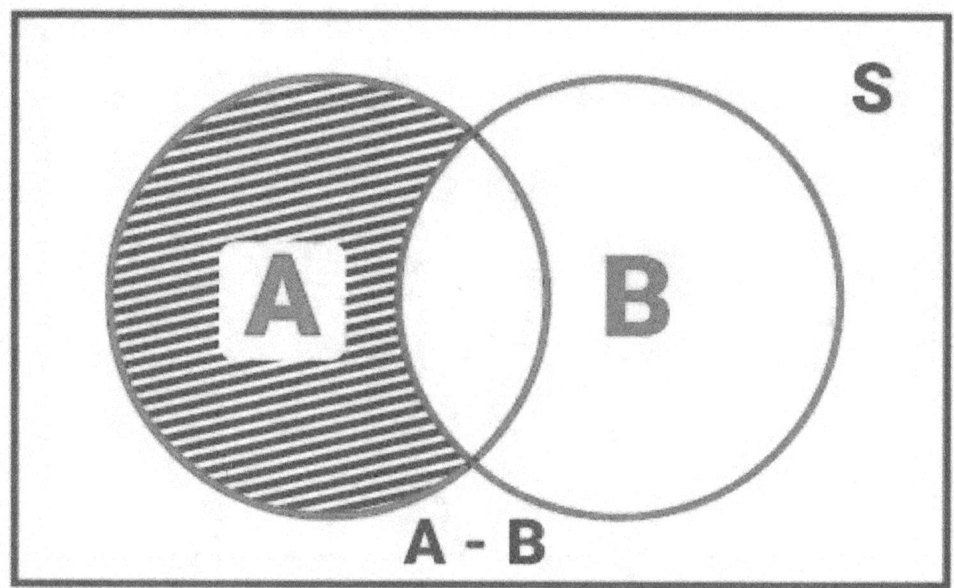

Fig.Ven diagramm for A-B

Let us consider the experiment of rolling a die.

The sample space is S = {1, 2, 3, 4, 5, 6}

Let A be the event of getting a prime number and B be the event of getting an even number.

The outcomes associated with these events are:

A = {2, 3, 5}

B = {2, 4, 6}

Thus, A − B = {2, 3, 5} − {2, 4, 6} = {3, 5}

Alternatively,

B′ = {1, 3, 5}

A ∩ B′ = { 2, 3, 5} ∩ {1, 3, 5} = {3, 5}

Therefore, A − B = {3, 5}

Solved Example

Question: Consider the experiment of throwing a die and the events are:

A: 'a number less than 4 appears',

B: 'a number greater than 2 but less than 5 appears'

Write the sets representing the events (i) A or B (ii) A and B (iii) A but not B (iv) 'not A' (v) 'not B'.

Solution:

Sample space = S = {1, 2, 3, 4, 5, 6}

A = {1, 2, 3}

B = {3, 4}

(i) A or B = A ∪ B = {1, 2, 3} ∪ {3, 4} = {1, 2, 3, 4}

(ii) A and B = A ∩ B = {1, 2, 3} ∩ {3, 4} = {3}

(iii) A but not B = A − B = {1, 2, 3} − {3, 4} = {1, 2}

(iv) not A = A′ = S − A = {1, 2, 3, 4, 5, 6} − {1, 2, 3} = {4, 5, 6}

(v) not B = B′ = S − B = {1, 2, 3, 4, 5, 6} − {3, 4} = {1, 2, 5, 6}

Independent Events and Dependent Events

If the occurrence of any event is completely unaffected by the occurrence of any other event, such events are known as an **independent event** in probability and the events which are affected by other events are known as **dependent events.**

Mutually Exclusive Events

If the occurrence of one event excludes the occurrence of another event, such events are mutually **exclusive events** i.e. two events don't have any common point. For example, if S = {1 , 2 , 3 , 4 , 5 , 6} and E_1, E_2 are two events such that E_1 consists of numbers less than 3 and E_2 consists of numbers greater than 4.

So, E1 = {1,2} and E2 = {5,6} .

Then, E1 and E2 are mutually exclusive.

Sets under the operations of union, intersection, and complement satisfy various laws (identities) which are listed below

Idempotent Laws

(a) $A \cup A = A$

(b) $A \cap A = A$

Associative Laws

(a) $(A \cup B) \cup C = A \cup (B \cup C)$

(b) $(A \cap B) \cap C = A \cap (B \cap C)$

Commutative Laws

(a) $A \cup B = B \cup A$

(b) $A \cap B = B \cap A$

Distributive Laws

(a) $A \cup (B \cap C) = (A \cup B) \cap (A \cup C)$

(b) $A \cap (B \cup C) = (A \cap B) \cup (A \cap C)$

De Morgan's Laws

(a) $(A \cup B)^c = A^c \cap B^c$

(b) $(A \cap B)^c = A^c \cup B^c$

Ex. In Throwing a fair dias,

A={The outcome is greater than 3}

B={The outcome is an even number}

Find $P(A)$, $P(B)$, $P(A|B)$, $P(A^c \cap B)$

We have A={4,5,6}, B={2,4,6} and A∩B={4,6}

$P(A) = 3/6 = 1/2$

$P(B) = 3/6 = 1/2$

$P(A \cap B) = 2/6 = 1/3$

Now, $P(A|B) = P(A \cap B)/P(B)$

$= (1/3)/(1/2)$

$= 2/3$

And $P(A^c \cap B) = P(B) - P(A \cap B) = (1/2) - (1/3) = 1/6$

Markov chain

A random process in which the occurrence of future state depends on the immediate preceding state and only on it known as Markov chain or process

Use of Markov chain:

1. Behaviour of consumer in terms of their brand loyalty and switching pattern
2. Machine use to manufacture a product [two state- working or not working at any point]

State: state is a condition or location of an object in the system at particular time.

Assumption:

1. Finite number of state
2. State are mutually exclusive
3. State are collectively exhaustive
4. Probability of moving from one state to other state is constant over time

Transition Probability:

The probability of moving from one state to another state or remaining in the same state during a single time period is called as transition probability

Mathematically defined it:

Pij = P (Next state Sj at t=1/initial state Si at t=0)

Here i is the initial state and j is the next state

Transition Probability Matrix (TPM) :

With the help of transition probability matrix, we predict the movement of system from one state to the next state.

$$P = \begin{bmatrix} P_{1,1} & P_{1,2} & \cdots & P_{1,j} & \cdots & P_{1,S} \\ P_{2,1} & P_{2,2} & \cdots & P_{2,j} & \cdots & P_{2,S} \\ \vdots & \vdots & \ddots & \vdots & \ddots & \vdots \\ P_{i,1} & P_{i,2} & \cdots & P_{i,j} & \cdots & P_{i,S} \\ \vdots & \vdots & \ddots & \vdots & \ddots & \vdots \\ P_{S,1} & P_{S,2} & \cdots & P_{S,j} & \cdots & P_{S,S} \end{bmatrix}.$$

Fig. Representation of Transition Probability Matrix

P11= P [in state S1 in at time t=1 / in state S1 at time=0]
P12= P [in state S2 in at time t=1 / in state S1 at time=0]
P21= P [in state S1 in at time t=1 / in state S2 at time=0]
* one step Transition Probability*
* Two step Transition Probability*
* n step Transition Probability*
TPM Assumption

1. Row sum=1
2. Each element of TPM is Probability 0 <= Pij <= 1 and non-Negative

3. Its always square matrix because

    Row shows- initial state
    Column Shows- alternate state in next move

Random Walk

A random walk can be defined as a series of discrete steps an object takes in some direction. Moreover, we determine the direction and movement of the object in each step probabilistically. In mathematics and probability theory, a random work is a random process.

In a random walk, the future position is entirely independent of the current position of an object. Additionally, it's an example of the Markov process. Starting from a position, the object can go in any direction. Each step taken by the object in any direction has a probability associated with it. Hence, the final position is completely independent of the point of origin.

A simple example of a random walk is a drunkard's walk. A drunk man has no preferential direction. Therefore, he's equally likely to move in all directions.

In the random work concept, the utmost significant problem is finding a probability distribution function that can estimate the probability of the current position of an object after taking a random walk for a fixed amount of time.

One Dimensional Random Walk

The simplest and basic random walk is a one-dimensional walk. **Let's look at a random walk on integers:**

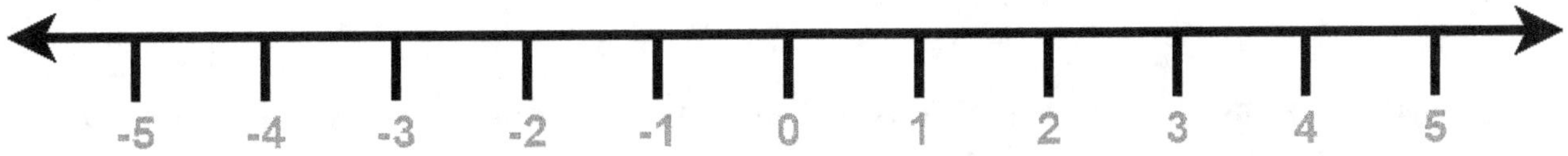

Enter Caption

So here, an object is standing at point 0. It can move in two directions: forwards and backward. Now we'll decide the direction of each step of the object by flipping a coin. In the case of a head, the object will move forward. If it's a tail, the object will move backward. Here we'll flip a coin, move the object one step according to the rule and flip the coin again.

Now let's start the process. Let's take the first turn:

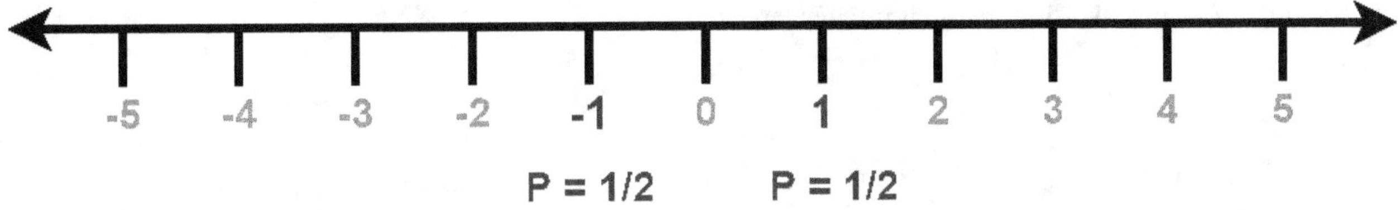

Enter Caption

After the first turn, the object can either go to +1 or -1 position with equal probability 1/2. Now let's take the second turn:

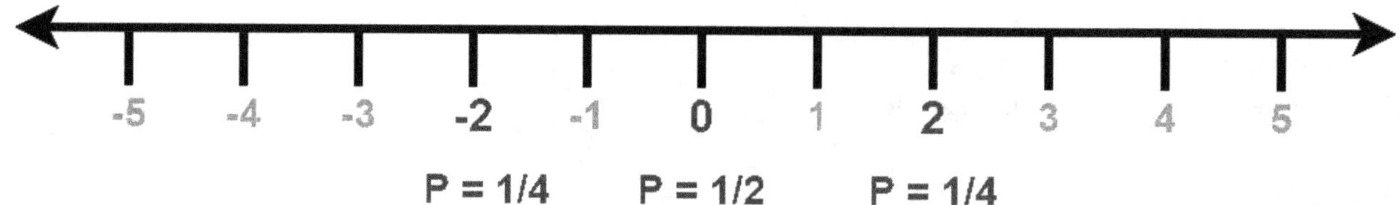

Enter Caption

After taking the second step, we can find the object in three positions: -2, 0 or +2. Here, the probability associated with positions 2 and -2 is the same. Although with the probability of 1/2, the object might be standing on the position 0. Likewise, let's look at the probabilities at the third turn:

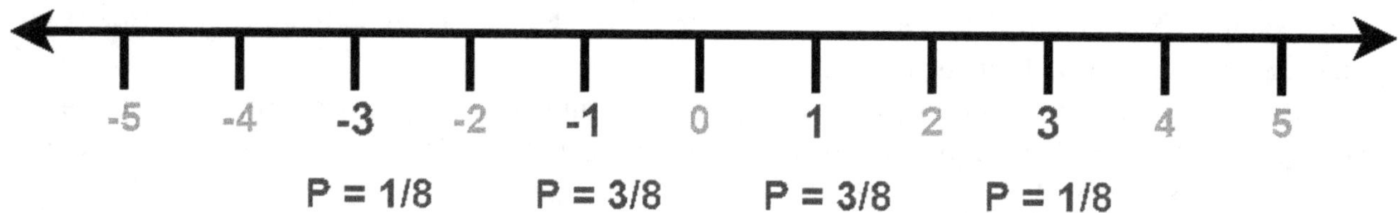

Enter Caption

Here the object can be found in -3, -1, 1, 3 positions. The probability of finding the object in either position 3or -3is 3/8. However, the probability of finding the object in either position 1or -1is 1/8.

Now it's easy to observe that when the number of turns is odd, all possible positions where the object can go is odd. Similarly, in the case of even turns, all possible positions are even numbers.

Now in order to get more insights from the one-dimensional random walk, let's assume C_j indicates the outcome of jth coin in the random process. Hence, C_1 is the outcome of the first coin flipped at the first turn. Additionally, the variable C_j is known as the random variable.

Now in the case of a one-dimensional random walk, the expected or average value of the random variable C_j is always 0.

Two-Dimensional Random Walk

A random walk can happen in any dimensional. We'll discuss the random walk in a two-dimensional integer lattice here. Let's look at a two-dimensional integer lattice

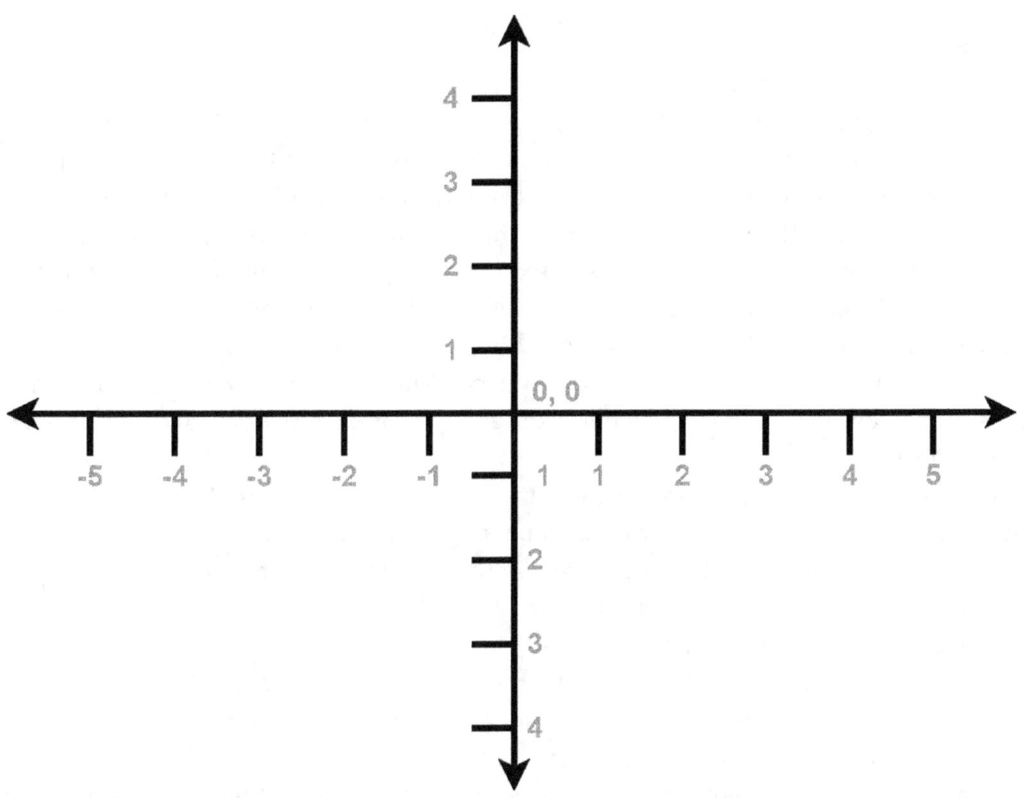

Enter Caption

In a two-dimensional random walk, an object can move in four different directions: forward, backward, left, right. Therefore, in this environment, in order to move the object, we need to flip a coin twice at each step. We can decide whether to move the object forward or backward in the first flip. The second flip will determine whether to go in the right or left direction.

Interestingly, in the random walk, the probability of reaching any point in the 2D grid is 1 when we set the number of steps to infinite.

Application of Random Walk

There're many applications of random walk in mathematics, computer science, biology, chemistry, physics. In biological genetic drift, random walks can give us a general idea of the statistical processes involved. In physics, we can use them to describe an ideal chain in polymer physics.

The random work concept is also crucial and used in several fields such as psychology, finance, ecology. Moreover, we can describe fluctuations in the share market with the random walk concept. Additionally, Google search engine algorithms also use them.

Flajolet Martin Algorithm:

Flajolet Martin Algorithm, also known as FM algorithm, is used to approximate the number of unique elements in a data stream or database in one pass. The highlight of this algorithm is that it uses less memory space while executing.

Pseudo Code-Stepwise Solution:

1. Selecting a hash function h so each element in the set is mapped to a string to at least $\log_2 n$ bits.
2. For each element x, r(x)= length of trailing zeroes in h(x)

3. R= max(r(x))

=> Distinct elements= 2^R

Reasons for using Flajolet Martin algorithm:

Let us compare this algorithm with our conventional algorithm using python code. Assume we have an array(stream in code) of data of length 20 with 8 unique elements. Using the brute force approach to find the number of unique elements in the array, each element is taken into consideration. Another array(st_unique in code) is formed for unique elements. Initially, the new array is empty(st_unique length equals zero), so naturally, the first element is not present in it. The first element is considered to be unique as it does not exist in the new array and thus a copy of the first element is inserted into the new array(1 is appended to st_unique).

Similarly, all the elements are checked, if they are already present in the new array, they are not considered to be unique, else a copy of the element is inserted into the new array. Running the brute force algorithm for our array, we will get 8 elements in the new array. If each element takes 20 bytes of data, the new array will take 8*20= 160 bytes memory to run the algorithm.

For the same array, if use the FM algorithm for the same array, we define a variable(maxnum in code) that stores the maximum number of zeroes at the end. For each value in the array(stream in code), we run a loop to covert its hash function in the form ax+b mod c,(a=1, b=6 and c=32 in this case) into binary(we place [2:] at the end because in python when converted to binary, the number starts with '0b'). We run another loop to find if the number of zeroes at the end exceeds the maximum number of zeroes.

In this case, if each variable occupies 2 bytes of data, the whole program takes 4*20= 80 bytes of data, i.e half of the memory used in the above case. Here, we have considered the variables maxnum, sum, val, and j. We have not considered i, time, and stream as they are common in both of the codes.

This is where the Flajolet Martin Algorithm can be used. Not only does it occupy less memory, but it also shows better results in terms of time in seconds when the python code is run which can be shown in our output as we calculated seconds taken by both algorithms by using time.time() in python. As shown in the output, it can clearly be said that the FM algorithm takes very little time as compared to the conventional algorithm.

Inputs

A static or stream bag (~ multiset) of integers.

X={1,3,5,7,5,2,7}

A hash function.

h(xi)=(3xi +1) mod 5

Steps of FM-algorithm

Step #1

x_i	$h(x_i)$
1	$(3 \cdot 1 + 1) \bmod 5 = 4$
3	$(3 \cdot 3 + 1) \bmod 5 = 0$
5	$(3 \cdot 5 + 1) \bmod 5 = 1$
7	$(3 \cdot 7 + 1) \bmod 5 = 2$
5	$(3 \cdot 5 + 1) \bmod 5 = 1$
2	$(3 \cdot 2 + 1) \bmod 5 = 2$
7	$(3 \cdot 7 + 1) \bmod 5 = 2$

Step #2

To write a binary representation of a hash value

x_i	$h(x_i)$	$binary(h(x_i))$
1	4	100
3	0	000
5	1	001
7	2	010
5	1	001
2	2	010
7	2	010

Enter Caption

Step #3

To calculate the count of trailing zeros in each binary representation of a hash value

x_i	$binary(h(x_i))$	r_i
1	100	2
3	000	0
5	001	0
7	010	1
5	001	0
2	010	1
7	010	1

Enter Caption

Step #4

Let's estimate **unique** elements by formula

$$R = 2^{max(r_i)} = 2^2 = 4$$

By fact, distinct values is 5. So, almost equal

Mean, Mode, Median, and Standard Deviation

Mean: The arithmetical mean is the sum of a set of numbers separated by the number of numbers in the collection, or simply the mean or the average.

To calculate the mean of a given data set, we use the following formula,

$$\bar{x} = \frac{1}{n} \sum_{i=1}^{n} x$$

where n is the sample size and the x correspond to the observed valued.

Example

Suppose you randomly sampled six acres in the Desolation Wilderness for a non-indigenous weed and came up with the following counts of this weed in this region:

34, 43, 81, 106, 106 and 115

We compute the sample mean by adding and dividing by the number of samples, 6.

$$\frac{34 + 43 + 81 + 106 + 106 + 115}{6} = 80.83$$

- **Mode:** The mode is the value that most frequently appears in a data value set. In the above example 106 is the mode, since it occurs twice and the rest of the outcomes occur only once.
- **Median:** In a sorted, ascending or descending, list of numbers, the median is the middle number and may be more representative of that data set than the average. If we have an even number of events we take the average of the two middles. The median is better for describing the typical value. It is often used for income and home prices.

Example

Suppose you randomly selected 10 house prices in the South Lake Tahoe area. Your are interested in the typical house price. In $100,000 the prices were

2.7, 2.9, 3.1, 3.4, 3.7, 4.1, 4.3, 4.7, 4.7, 40.8

If we computed the mean, we would say that the average house price is 744,000. Although this number is true, it does not reflect the price for available housing in South Lake Tahoe. A closer look at the data shows that the house valued at 40.8 x $100,000 = $4.08 million skews the data. Instead, we use the median. Since there is an even number of outcomes, we take the average of the middle two

$$\frac{3.7 + 4.1}{2} = 3.9$$

The median house price is $390,000. This better reflects what house shoppers should expect to spend.

Variance, Standard Deviation

The mean, mode, median, and trimmed mean do a nice job in telling where the centre of the data set is, but often we are interested in more. For example, a pharmaceutical engineer develops a new drug that regulates iron in the blood. Suppose she finds out that the average sugar content after taking the medication is the optimal level. This does not mean that the drug is effective. There is a possibility that half of the patients have dangerously low sugar content while the other half have dangerously high content. Instead of the drug being an effective regulator, it is a deadly poison. What the pharmacist needs is a measure of how far the data is spread apart. This is what the variance and standard deviation do. First we show the formulas for these measurements. Then we will go through the steps on how to use the formulas.

We define the *variance* to be

$$s^2 = \frac{1}{n-1} \sum_{i=1}^{n} (x - \bar{x})^2$$

and the *standard deviation* to be

$$s = \sqrt{\frac{1}{n-1} \sum_{i=1}^{n} (x - \bar{x})^2}$$

Enter Caption

Mean, Mode, Median, and Standard Deviation

The Mean and Mode

The *sample mean* is the average and is computed as the sum of all the observed outcomes from the sample divided by the total number of events. We use x as the symbol for the sample mean. In math terms,

$$\bar{x} = \frac{1}{n} \sum_{i=1}^{n} x$$

where n is the sample size and the x correspond to the observed valued.

Example

Suppose you randomly sampled six acres in the Desolation Wilderness for a non-indigenous weed and came up with the following counts of this weed in this region:

34, 43, 81, 106, 106 and 115

We compute the sample mean by adding and dividing by the number of samples, 6.

34 + 43 + 81 + 106 + 106 + 115
-- = 80.83
6

We can say that the sample mean of non-indigenous weed is 80.83.

The *mode* of a set of data is the number with the highest frequency. In the above example 106 is the mode, since it occurs twice and the rest of the outcomes occur only once.

The *population mean* isthe average of the entire population and is usually impossible to compute. We use the Greek letter m for the population mean.

Median, and Trimmed Mean

One problem with using the mean, is that it often does not depict the typical outcome. If there is one outcome that is very far from the rest of the data, then the mean will be strongly affected by this outcome. Such an outcome is called and *outlier*. An alternative measure is the median. The *median* is the middle score. If we have an even number of events we take the average of the two middles. The median is better for describing the typical value. It is often used for income and home prices.

Example

Suppose you randomly selected 10 house prices in the South Lake Tahoe area. Your are interested in the typical house price. In $100,000 the prices were

2.7, 2.9, 3.1, 3.4, 3.7, 4.1, 4.3, 4.7, 4.7, 40.8

If we computed the mean, we would say that the average house price is 744,000. Although this number is true, it does not reflect the price for available housing in South Lake Tahoe. A closer look at the data shows that the house valued at 40.8 x $100,000 = $4.08 million skews the data. Instead, we use the median. Since there is an even number of outcomes, we take the average of the middle two

$$\frac{3.7 + 4.1}{2} = 3.9$$

The median house price is $390,000. This better reflects what house shoppers should expect to spend. There is an alternative value that also is resistant to outliers. This is called the *trimmed mean* which is the mean after getting rid of the outliers or 5% on the top and 5% on the bottom. We can also use the trimmed mean if we are concerned with outliers skewing the data, however the median is used more often since more people understand it.

Example:

At a ski rental shop data was collected on the number of rentals on each of ten consecutive Saturdays:

44, 50, 38, 96, 42, 47, 40, 39, 46, 50.

To find the sample mean, add them and divide by 10:

$$\frac{44 + 50 + 38 + 96 + 42 + 47 + 40 + 39 + 46 + 50}{10} = 49.2$$

Notice that the mean value is not a value of the sample.

To find the median, first sort the data:

38, 39, 40, 42, 44, 46, 47, 50, 50, 96

Notice that there are two middle numbers 44 and 46. To find the median we take the average of the two.

$$\text{Median} = \frac{44 + 46}{2} = 45$$

Notice also that the mean is larger than all but three of the data points. The mean is influenced by outliers while the median is robust.

Correlation Coefficient

Correlation coefficient formulas are used to find how strong a relationship is between data. The formulas return a value between -1 and 1, where:

- 1 indicates a strong positive relationship.
- -1 indicates a strong negative relationship.
- A result of zero indicates no relationship at all.

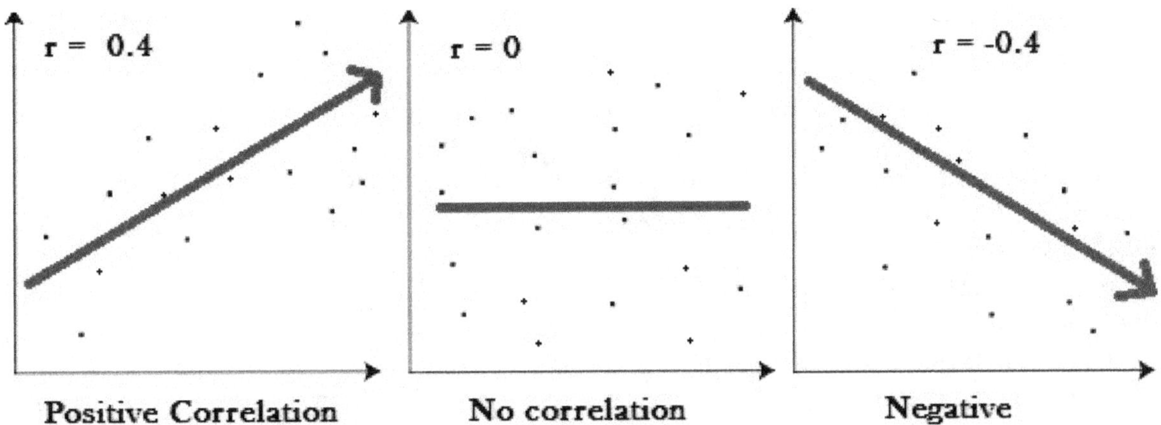

Fig. Correlation

- A correlation coefficient of 1 means that for every positive increase in one variable, there is a positive increase of a fixed proportion in the other. For example, shoe sizes go up in (almost) perfect correlation with foot length.
- A correlation coefficient of -1 means that for every positive increase in one variable, there is a negative decrease of a fixed proportion in the other. For example, the amount of gas in a tank decreases in (almost) perfect correlation with speed.
- Zero means that for every increase, there isn't a positive or negative increase. The two just aren't related. The absolute value of the correlation coefficient gives us the relationship strength. The larger the number, the stronger the relationship. **For example, |-.75| = .75, which has a stronger relationship than .65.**
- There are several types of correlation coefficient formulas.

One of the most commonly used formulas is Pearson's correlation coefficient formula. If you're taking a basic stats class, this is the one you'll probably use:

Types of correlation coefficient formulas.

$$r = \frac{n(\Sigma xy) - (\Sigma x)(\Sigma y)}{\sqrt{[\,n\Sigma x^2 - (\Sigma x)^2\,][\,n\Sigma y^2 - (\Sigma y)^2\,]}}$$

Example question: Find the value of the correlation coefficient from the following table

SUBJECT AGE X GLUCOSE LEVEL Y
1 43 99

2 21 65

3 25 79

4 42 75

5 57 87

6 59 81

Make a chart. Use the given data, and add three more columns: xy, x2, and y2.

SUBJECT AGE X GLUCOSE LEVEL Y XY X2 Y2

1 43 99 4257 1849 9801

2 21 65 1365 441 4225

3 25 79 1975 625 6241

4 42 75 3150 1764 5625

5 57 87 4959 3249 7569

6 59 81 4779 3481 6561

Σ 247 486 20485 11409 40022

From our table:

- $\Sigma x = 247$

  $\Sigma y = 486$

  $\Sigma xy = 20,485$

  $\Sigma x2 = 11,409$

  $\Sigma y2 = 40,022$

  n is the sample size, in our case = 6

  The correlation coefficient =

  $=6(20,485) - (247 \times 486) / [\sqrt{[[6(11,409) - (2472)] \times [6(40,022) - 4862]]]}$

  = 0.5298

The range of the correlation coefficient is from -1 to 1. Our result is 0.5298 or 52.98%, which means the variables have a moderate positive correlation.\

Analysis of variance (ANOVA)

Buying a new product or testing a new technique but not sure how it stacks up against the alternatives? It's an all too familiar situation for most of us. Most of the options sound similar to each other so picking the best out of the lot is a challenge.

Consider a scenario where we have three medical treatments to apply on patients with similar diseases. Once we have the test results, one approach is to assume that the treatment which took the least time to cure the patients is the best among them. What if some of these patients had already been partially cured, or if any other medication was already working on them?

In order to make a confident and reliable decision, we will need evidence to support our approach. This is where the concept of ANOVA comes into play.

A common approach to figure out a reliable treatment method would be to analyse the days it took the patients to be cured. We can use a statistical technique which can compare these three treatment samples and depict how different these samples are from one another. Such a technique, which compares the samples on the basis of their means, is called ANOVA.

Analysis of variance (ANOVA) is a statistical technique that is used to check if the means of two or more groups are significantly different from each other. ANOVA checks the impact of one or more factors by comparing the means of different samples.

One-Way ANOVA Versus Two-Way ANOVA

There are two main types of ANOVA: one-way (or unidirectional) and two-way. There also variations of ANOVA. For example, MANOVA (multivariate ANOVA) differs from ANOVA as the former tests for multiple dependent variables simultaneously while the latter assesses only one dependent variable at a time. One-way or two-way refers to the number of independent variables in your analysis of variance test. A one-way ANOVA evaluates the impact of a sole factor on a sole response variable. It determines whether all the samples are the same. The one-way ANOVA is used to determine whether there are any statistically significant differences between the means of three or more independent (unrelated) groups.

A two-way ANOVA is an extension of the one-way ANOVA. With a one-way, you have one independent variable affecting a dependent variable. With a two-way ANOVA, there are two independents. For example, a two-way ANOVA allows a company to compare worker productivity based on two independent variables, such as salary and skill set. It is utilized to observe the interaction between the two factors and tests the effect of two factors at the same time.

## CHAPTER THREE

Big Data Processing

Big data ecosystem

Big data ecosystem is the comprehension of massive functional components with various enabling tools. Capabilities of the big data ecosystem are not only about computing and storing big data, but also the advantages of its systematic platform and potentials of big data analytics.

Consumption
Analysis
Storage
Ingestion

Fig. Components of Big Data Ecosystem

Data Sources/Ingestion

The ingestion layer is the very first step of pulling in raw data. It comes from internal sources, relational databases, nonrelational databases and others, etc. It can even come from social media, emails, phone calls or somewhere else. There are two kinds of data ingestion:

1. Batch, in which large groups of data are gathered and delivered together. Data collection can be triggered by conditions, launched on a schedule or ad hoc.
2. Streaming, which is a continuous flow of data. This is necessary for real-time data analytics. It locates and pulls data as it's generated. This requires more resources because it is constantly monitoring for changes in data pools.

Storage

This is where the converted data is stored in a data lake or warehouse and eventually processed. It's the actual embodiment of big data: a huge set of usable, homogenous data, as opposed to simply a large collection of random, incohesive data.

Many consider the data lake/warehouse the most essential component of a big data ecosystem. It needs to contain only thorough, relevant data to make insights as valuable as possible. It must be efficient with as little redundancy as possible to allow for quicker processing. It needs to be accessible with a large output bandwidth for the same reason.

Lakes differ from warehouses in that they preserve the original raw data, meaning little has been done in the transformation stage other than data quality assurance and redundancy reduction. Comparatively, data stored in a warehouse is much more focused on the specific task of analysis, and is consequently much less useful for other analysis efforts. Because of the focus, warehouses store much less data and typically produce quicker results.

Analysis

Analysis is the big data component where all the dirty work happens. In the analysis layer, data gets passed through several tools, shaping it into actionable insights.

There are four types of analytics on big data: diagnostic, descriptive, predictive and prescriptive.

- Diagnostic: Explains why a problem is happening. Big data allows analytics to take a deep dive into things like customer information, marketing metrics and key performance indicators to explain why certain actions didn't produce the expected results. Projects are undertaken with an expectation of certain results based on certain estimations of markets, customers and other similar criteria. Diagnostic analytics digs into which assumed contributors didn't meet their projected metrics.
- Descriptive: Describes the current state of a business through historical data. It uses previous trends to forecast things like sales rates, seasonal impacts and more. In big data, the use of far-reaching market data and customer insights help contextualize internal metrics and increase the intelligence of a business's position amongst its competitors. In boiled down terms, it answers "what" questions.
- Predictive: Projects future results based on historical data. By highlighting patterns and evaluating trajectories of relevant metrics, predictive analytics estimates future efforts.
- Prescriptive: Takes predictive analytics a step further by projecting best future efforts. By tweaking inputs and changing actions, prescriptive analytics allows businesses to decide how to put their best foot forward. Different actions will yield different results, and prescriptive analytics helps decision makers try to decide the best way to proceed.

Consumption

The final big data component involves presenting the information in a format digestible to the end-user. This can materialize in the forms of tables, advanced visualizations and even single numbers if requested. This is what businesses use to pull the trigger on new processes.

The most important thing in this layer is making sure the intent and meaning of the output is understandable. Up until this point, every person actively involved in the process has been a data scientist, or at least literate in data science. But in the consumption layer, executives and decision-makers enter the picture. They need to be able to interpret what the data is saying.

There's a robust category of distinct products for this stage, known as enterprise reporting. That's how essential it is. Visualizations come in the form of real-time dashboards, charts, graphs, graphics and maps, just to name a few. Many rely on mobile and cloud capabilities so that data is accessible from anywhere.

Google File System (GFS)

Google File System (GFS) is a scalable distributed file system (DFS) created by Google Inc. and developed to accommodate Google's expanding data processing requirements. GFS provides fault tolerance, reliability, scalability, availability and performance to large networks and connected nodes. GFS is made up of several storage systems built from low-cost commodity hardware components. It is optimized to accomodate Google's different data use and storage needs, such as its search engine, which generates huge amounts of data that must be stored.

The Google File System capitalized on the strength of off-the-shelf servers while minimizing hardware weaknesses.

The GFS node cluster is a single master with multiple chunk servers that are continuously accessed by different client systems. Chunk servers store data as Linux files on local disks. Stored data is divided into large chunks (64

MB), which are replicated in the network a minimum of three times. The large chunk size reduces network overhead.

GFS is designed to accommodate Google's large cluster requirements without burdening applications. Files are stored in hierarchical directories identified by path names. Metadata - such as namespace, access control data, and mapping information - is controlled by the master, which interacts with and monitors the status updates of each chunk server through timed heartbeat messages.

GFS features include:

1. Fault tolerance
2. Critical data replication
3. Automatic and efficient data recovery
4. High aggregate throughput
5. Reduced client and master interaction because of large chunk server size
6. Namespace management and locking
7. High availability

The largest GFS clusters have more than 1,000 nodes with 300 TB disk storage capacity. This can be accessed by hundreds of clients on a continuous basis.

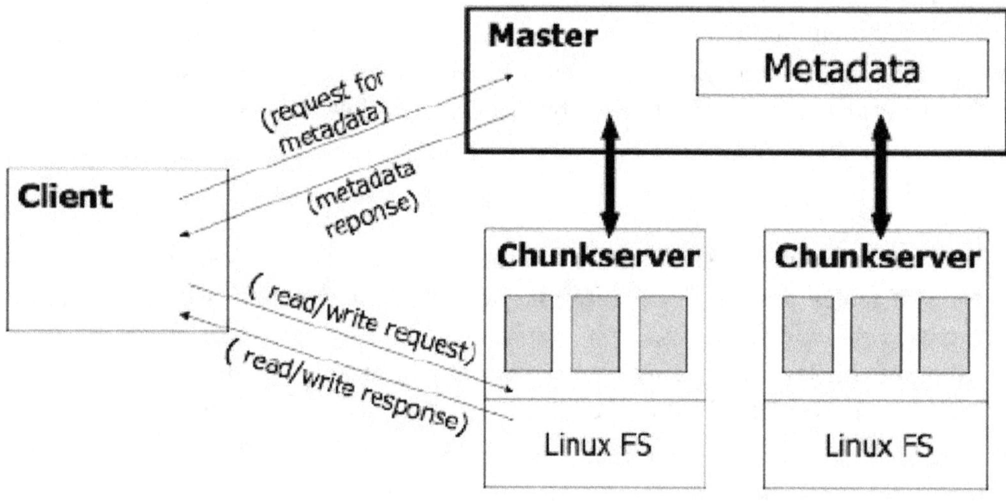

Fig.GFS Architecture

FS is clusters of computers. A cluster is simply a network of computers. Each cluster might contain hundreds or even thousands of machines. In each GFS clusters there are three main entities:

1. Clients
2. Master servers
3. Chunk servers.

Client can be other computers or computer applications and make a file request. Requests can range from retrieving and manipulating existing files to creating new files on the system. Clients can be thought as customers of the GFS.

Master Server is the coordinator for the cluster. Its task include:-

- Maintaining an operation log, that keeps track of the activities of the cluster. The operation log helps keep service interruptions to a minimum if the master server crashes, a replacement server that has monitored the operation log can take its place.
- The master server also keeps track of metadata, which is the information that describes chunks. The metadata tells the master server to which files the chunks belong and where they fit within the overall file.

Chunk Servers are the workhorses of the GFS. They store 64-MB file chunks. The chunk servers don't send chunks to the master server. Instead, they send requested chunks directly to the client. The GFS copies every chunk multiple times and stores it on different chunk servers. Each copy is called a replica. By default, the GFS makes three replicas per chunk, but users can change the setting and make more or fewer replicas if desired.

Hadoop

Hadoop is an open source framework from Apache and is used to store process and analyze data which are very huge in volume. Hadoop is written in Java and is not OLAP (online analytical processing). It is used for batch/offline processing. It is being used by Facebook, Yahoo, Google, Twitter, LinkedIn and many more. Moreover it can be scaled up just by adding nodes in the cluster.

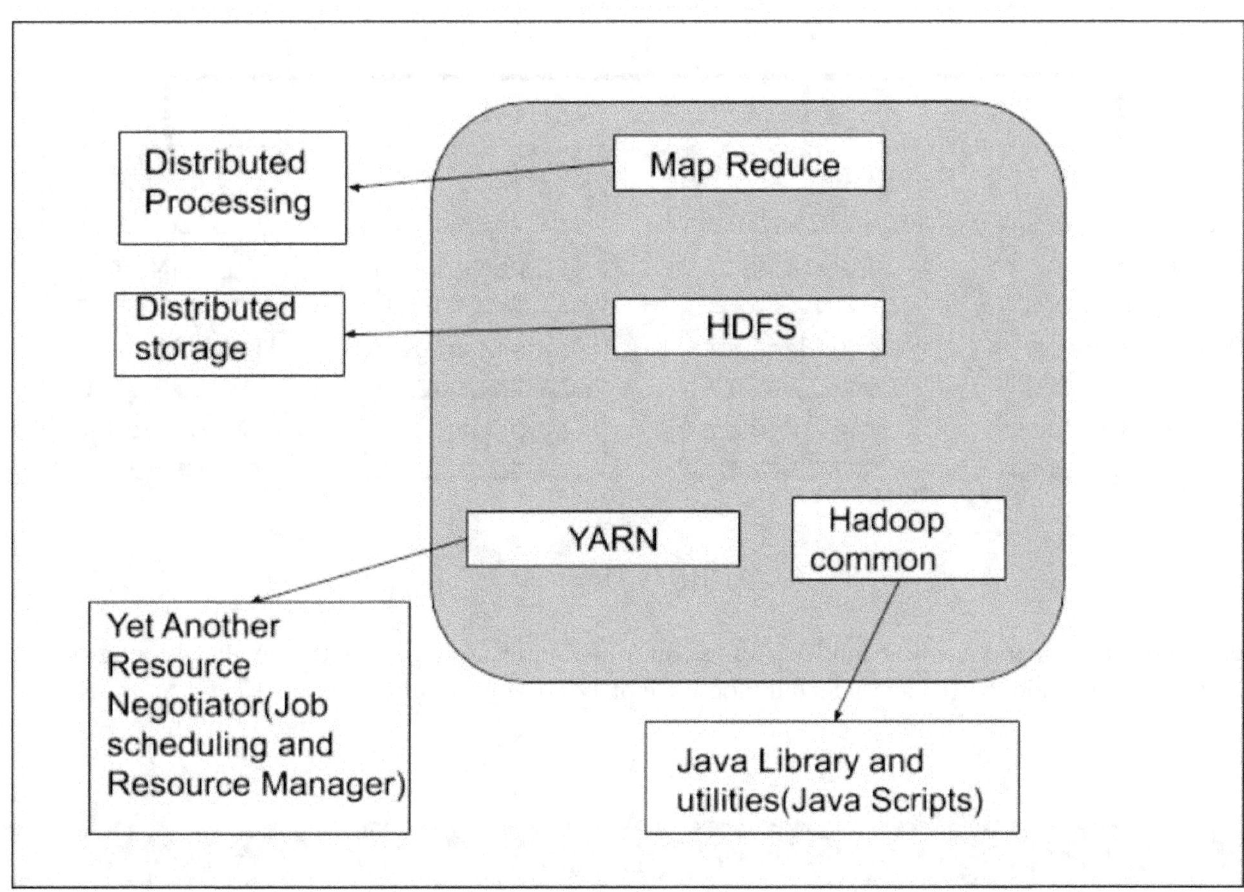

Fig. Hadoop – Architecture

HDFS: Hadoop Distributed File System. Google published its paper GFS and on the basis of that HDFS was developed. It states that the files will be broken into blocks and stored in nodes over the distributed architecture. It has got two daemons running. One for master node – NameNode and other for slave nodes – DataNode.

a. NameNode and DataNode

HDFS has a Master-slave architecture. The daemon called NameNode runs on the master server. It is responsible for Namespace management and regulates file access by the client. DataNode daemon runs on slave nodes. It is responsible for storing actual business data. Internally, a file gets split into a number of data blocks and stored on a group of slave machines. Namenode manages modifications to file system namespace. These are actions like the opening, closing and renaming files or directories. NameNode also keeps track of mapping of blocks to DataNodes. This DataNodes serves read/write request from the file system's client. DataNode also creates, deletes and replicates blocks on demand from NameNode.

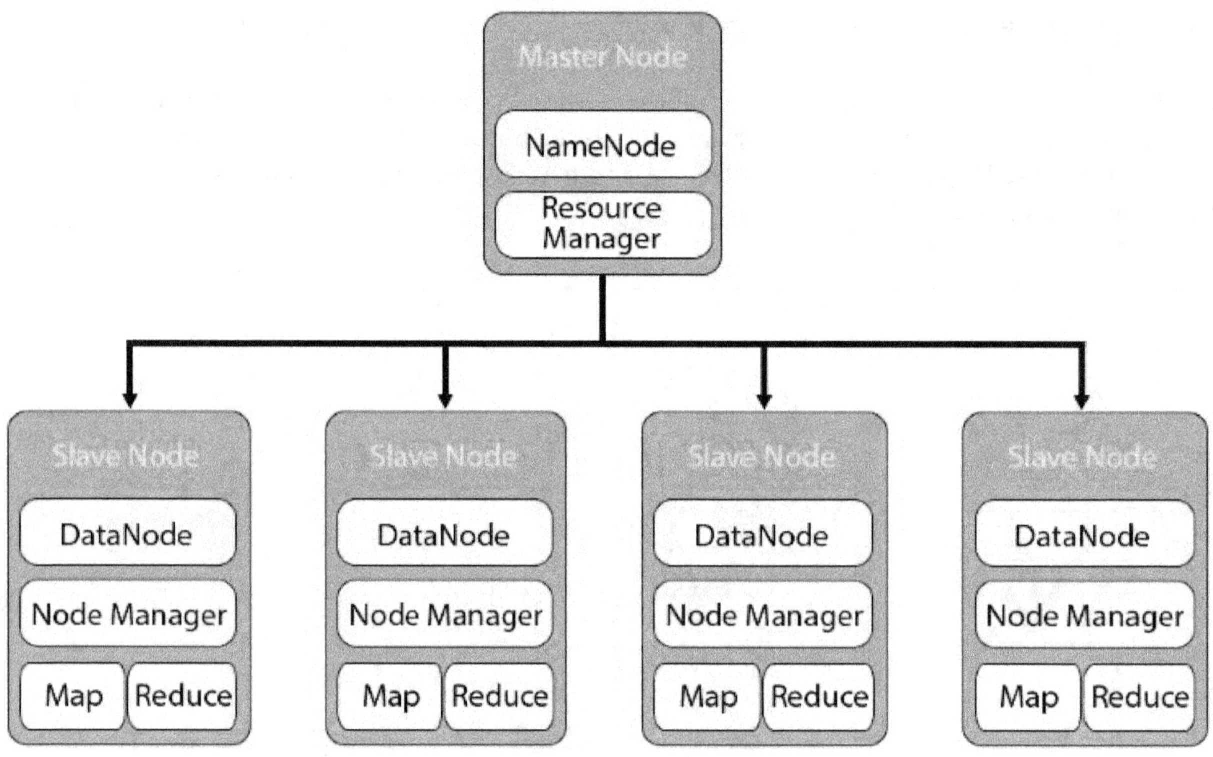

Fig.HDFS Architecture

Block is nothing but the smallest unit of storage on a computer system. It is the smallest contiguous storage allocated to a file. In Hadoop, we have a default block size of 128MB or 256MB.

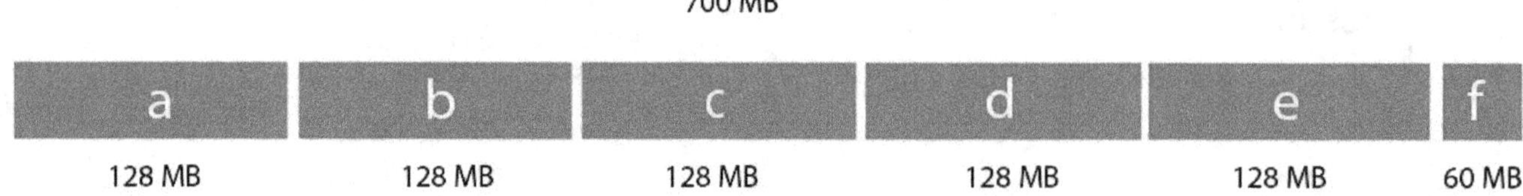

One should select the block size very carefully. To explain why so let us take an example of a file which is 700MB in size. If our block size is 128MB then HDFS divides the file into 6 blocks. Five blocks of 128MB and one block of 60MB. What will happen if the block is of size 4KB? But in HDFS we would be having files of size in the order terabytes to petabytes. With 4KB of the block size, we would be having numerous blocks. This, in turn, will create huge metadata which will overload the NameNode. Hence we have to choose our HDFS block size judiciously.

c. Replication Management

To provide fault tolerance HDFS uses a replication technique. In that, it makes copies of the blocks and stores in on different DataNodes. Replication factor decides how many copies of the blocks get stored. It is 3 by default but we can configure to any value. Suppose we have a file of 1GB then with a replication factor of 3 it will require 3GBs of total storage.

Yarn: YARN or Yet Another Resource Negotiator is the resource management layer of Hadoop. The basic principle behind YARN is to separate resource management and job scheduling/monitoring function into separate daemons. In YARN there is one global Resource Manager and per-application Application Master. An Application can be a single job or a DAG of jobs.

Inside the YARN framework, we have two daemons Resource Manager and Node Manager. The Resource Manager arbitrates resources among all the competing applications in the system. The job of Node Manager is to monitor the resource usage by the container and report the same to Resource Manager. The resources are like CPU, memory, disk, network and so on.

Map Reduce: MapReduce is the data processing layer of Hadoop. It is a software framework that allows you to write applications for processing a large amount of data. MapReduce runs these applications in parallel on a cluster of low-end machines. It does so in a reliable and fault-tolerant manner.

MapReduce job comprises a number of map tasks and reduces tasks. Each task works on a part of data. This distributes the load across the cluster. The function of Map tasks is to load, parse, transform and filter data. Each reduce task works on the sub-set of output from the map tasks. Reduce task applies grouping and aggregation to this intermediate data from the map tasks.

The input file for the MapReduce job exists on HDFS. The input format decides how to split the input file into input splits. Input split is nothing but a byte-oriented view of the chunk of the input file. This input split gets loaded by the map task. The map task runs on the node where the relevant data is present. The data need not move over the network and get processed locally.

Hadoop Common: These Java libraries are used to start Hadoop and are used by other Hadoop modules.

HDFS Common Hadoop Shell Command:

HDFS is the primary or major component of the Hadoop ecosystem which is responsible for storing large data sets of structured or unstructured data across various nodes and thereby maintaining the metadata in the form of log files. To use the HDFS commands, first you need to start the Hadoop services using the following command:

Start -dfs

Start -yarn

To check the Hadoop services are up and running use the following command:

Jps

Create a directory in HDFS at given path(s).

Usage:

hadoop fs -mkdir <paths> Example:

hadoop fs -mkdir /user/saurzcode/dir1 /user/saurzcode/dir2

List the contents of a directory.

Usage :

hadoop fs -ls <args> Example:

hadoop fs -ls /user/saurzcode

Upload and download a file in HDFS.

Upload: **hadoop fs -put:**
  Copy single src file, or multiple src files from local file system to the Hadoop data file system
  Usage:
  hadoop fs -put <localsrc> ... <HDFS_dest_Path> Example:
  hadoop fs -put /home/saurzcode/Samplefile.txt /user/ saurzcode/dir3/
  Download:
  hadoop fs -get:
  Copies/Downloads files to the local file system
  Usage:
  hadoop fs -get <hdfs_src> <localdst> Example:
  hadoop fs -get /user/saurzcode/dir3/Samplefile.txt /home/

See contents of a file

Same as unix cat command:
  Usage:
  hadoop fs -cat <path[filename]> Example:
  hadoop fs -cat /user/saurzcode/dir1/abc.txt

Copy a file from source to destination

This command allows multiple sources as well in which case the destination must be a directory.
  Usage:
  hadoop fs -cp <source> <dest> Example:
  hadoop fs -cp /user/saurzcode/dir1/abc.txt /user/saurzcode/ dir2

Copy a file from/To Local file system to HDFS

copyFromLocal
  Usage:
  hadoop fs -copyFromLocal <localsrc> URI Example:
  hadoop fs -copyFromLocal /home/saurzcode/abc.txt /user/ saurzcode/abc.txt
  Similar to put command, except that the source is restricted to a local file reference.
  copyToLocal
  Usage:
  hadoop fs -copyToLocal [-ignorecrc] [-crc] URI <localdst>
  Similar to get command, except that the destination is restricted to a local file reference.
  Move file from source to destination.
  Note:- Moving files across filesystem is not permitted.
  Usage :
  hadoop fs -mv <src> <dest> Example:
  hadoop fs -mv /user/saurzcode/dir1/abc.txt /user/saurzcode/ dir2

Remove a file or directory in HDFS.

Remove files specified as argument. Deletes directory only when it is empty
    Usage :
    hadoop fs -rm <arg> Example:
    hadoop fs -rm /user/saurzcode/dir1/abc.txt
    Recursive version of delete.
    Usage :
    hadoop fs -rmr <arg> Example:
    hadoop fs -rmr /user/saurzcode/

Display last few lines of a file.

Similar to tail command in Unix.
    Usage :
    hadoop fs -tail <path[filename]> Example:
    hadoop fs -tail /user/saurzcode/dir1/abc.txt

Display the aggregate length of a file.

Usage :
    hadoop fs -du <path> Example:
    hadoop fs -du /user/saurzcode/dir1/abc.txt

Hadoop MapReduce Paradigm

MapReduce is a processing technique and a program model for distributed computing based on java. The MapReduce algorithm contains two important tasks, namely Map and Reduce. Map takes a set of data and converts it into another set of data, where individual elements are broken down into tuples (key/value pairs). Secondly, reduce task, which takes the output from a map as an input and combines those data tuples into a smaller set of tuples. As the sequence of the name MapReduce implies, the reduce task is always performed after the map job.

The major advantage of MapReduce is that it is easy to scale data processing over multiple computing nodes. Under the MapReduce model, the data processing primitives are called mappers and reducers. Decomposing a data processing application into *mappers* and *reducers* is sometimes nontrivial. But, once we write an application in the MapReduce form, scaling the application to run over hundreds, thousands, or even tens of thousands of machines in a cluster is merely a configuration change. This simple scalability is what has attracted many programmers to use the MapReduce model.

The Algorithm

- Generally MapReduce paradigm is based on sending the computer to where the data resides!
- MapReduce program executes in three stages, namely map stage, shuffle stage, and reduce stage.

  - **Map stage** – The map or mapper's job is to process the input data. Generally the input data is in the form of file or directory and is stored in the Hadoop file system (HDFS). The input file is passed to the mapper function

line by line. The mapper processes the data and creates several small chunks of data.
- ○ **Reduce stage** – This stage is the combination of the **Shuffle** stage and the **Reduce** stage. The Reducer's job is to process the data that comes from the mapper. After processing, it produces a new set of output, which will be stored in the HDFS.

- During a MapReduce job, Hadoop sends the Map and Reduce tasks to the appropriate servers in the cluster.
- The framework manages all the details of data-passing such as issuing tasks, verifying task completion, and copying data around the cluster between the nodes.
- Most of the computing takes place on nodes with data on local disks that reduces the network traffic.
- After completion of the given tasks, the cluster collects and reduces the data to form an appropriate result, and sends it back to the Hadoop server.

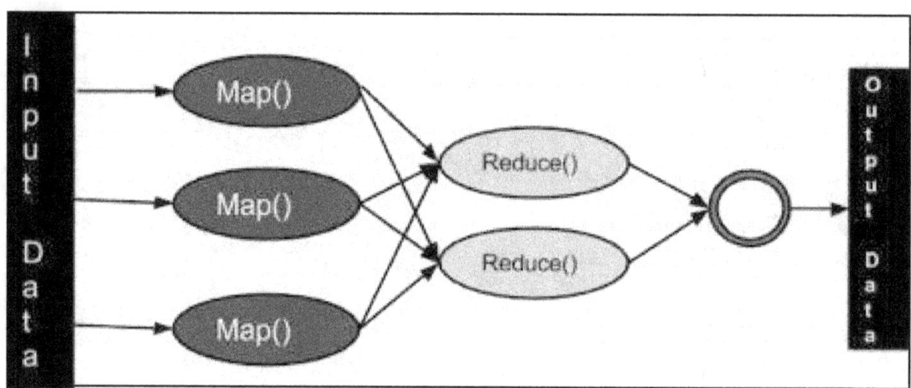

Fig. MapReduce Paradigm

JobTracker and TaskTracker

JobTracker and TaskTracker are 2 essential process involved in MapReduce execution in MRv1 (or Hadoop version 1). Both processes are now deprecated in MRv2 (or Hadoop version 2) and replaced by Resource Manager/Application Master and Node Manager Daemons.

Job Tracker –
- Job Tracker process runs on a separate node and not usually on a DataNode.
- Job Tracker is an essential Daemon for MapReduce execution in MRv1. It is replaced by Resource Manager/ Application Master in MRv2.
- **TaskTracker –**
- Task Tracker runs on DataNode. Mostly on all DataNodes.
- Task Tracker is replaced by Node Manager in MRv2.
- Mapper and Reducer tasks are executed on DataNodes administered by Task Trackers.
- Task Trackers will be assigned Mapper and Reducer tasks to execute by Job Tracker.
- Task Tracker will be in constant communication with the Job Tracker signalling the progress of the task in execution.
- Task Tracker failure is not considered fatal. When a Task Tracker becomes unresponsive, Job Tracker will assign the task executed by the Task Tracker to another node.
-
- Job Tracker receives the requests for MapReduce execution from the client.
- Job Tracker talks to the NameNode to determine the location of the data.
- Job Tracker finds the best Task Tracker nodes to execute tasks based on the data locality (proximity of the data) and the available slots to execute a task on a given node.

- Job Tracker monitors the individual Task Trackers and the submits back the overall status of the job back to the client.
- Job Tracker process is critical to the Hadoop cluster in terms of MapReduce execution.
- When the Job Tracker is down, HDFS will still be functional but the MapReduce execution cannot be started and the existing MapReduce jobs will be halted.

Introduction to NoSQL

A NoSQL originally referring to non SQL or non relational is a database that provides a mechanism for storage and retrieval of data. This data is modeled in means other than the tabular relations used in relational databases. NoSQL databases are used in real-time web applications and big data and their use are increasing over time. NoSQL systems are also sometimes called Not only SQL to emphasize the fact that they may support SQL-like query languages.

A NoSQL database includes simplicity of design, simpler horizontal scaling to clusters of machines and finer control over availability. The data structures used by NoSQL databases are different from those used by default in relational databases which makes some operations faster in NoSQL. The suitability of a given NoSQL database depends on the problem it should solve. Data structures used by NoSQL databases are sometimes also viewed as more flexible than relational database tables.

Most NoSQL databases offer a concept of eventual consistency in which database changes are propagated to all nodes so queries for data might not return updated data immediately or might result in reading data that is not accurate which is a problem known as stale reads

Advantages of NoSQL:

There are many advantages of working with NoSQL databases such as MongoDB and Cassandra. The main advantages are high scalability and high availability.

1. High scalability –

NoSQL database use sharding for horizontal scaling. Partitioning of data and placing it on multiple machines in such a way that the order of the data is preserved is sharding. Vertical scaling means adding more resources to the existing machine whereas horizontal scaling means adding more machines to handle the data. Vertical scaling is not that easy to implement but horizontal scaling is easy to implement. Examples of horizontal scaling databases are MongoDB, Cassandra etc. NoSQL can handle huge amount of data because of scalability, as the data grows NoSQL scale itself to handle that data in efficient manner.

1. High availability –

Auto replication feature in NoSQL databases makes it highly available because in case of any failure data replicates itself to the previous consistent state.

Disadvantages of NoSQL:

NoSQL has the following disadvantages.

1. Narrow focus –

NoSQL databases have very narrow focus as it is mainly designed for storage but it provides very little functionality. Relational databases are a better choice in the field of Transaction Management than NoSQL.

2. Open-source –

NoSQL is open-source database. There is no reliable standard for NoSQL yet. In other words two database systems are likely to be unequal.

3. Management challenge –

The purpose of big data tools is to make management of a large amount of data as simple as possible. But it is not so easy. Data management in NoSQL is much more complex than a relational database. NoSQL, in particular, has a reputation for being challenging to install and even more hectic to manage on a daily basis.

4. GUI is not available –

GUI mode tools to access the database is not flexibly available in the market.

5. Backup –

Backup is a great weak point for some NoSQL databases like MongoDB. MongoDB has no approach for the backup of data in a consistent manner.

6. Large document size –

Some database systems like MongoDB and CouchDB store data in JSON format. Which means that documents are quite large (BigData, network bandwidth, speed), and having descriptive key names actually hurts, since they increase the document size.

Difference between SQL and NoSQL

1. Type –

SQL databases are primarily called as Relational Databases (RDBMS); whereas NoSQL database are primarily called as non-relational or distributed database.

2. Language –

SQL databases defines and manipulates data based structured query language (SQL). Seeing from a side this language is extremely powerful. SQL is one of the most versatile and widely-used options available which makes it a safe choice especially for great complex queries. But from other side it can be restrictive. SQL requires you to use predefined schemas to determine the structure of your data before you work with it. Also all of your data must follow the same structure. This can require significant up-front preparation which means that a change in the structure would be both difficult and disruptive to your whole system.

A NoSQL database has dynamic schema for unstructured data. Data is stored in many ways which means it can be document-oriented, column-oriented, graph-based or organized as a KeyValue store. This flexibility means that documents can be created without having defined structure first. Also each document can have its own unique structure. The syntax varies from database to database, and you can add fields as you go.

3. The Scalability –

In almost all situations SQL databases are vertically scalable. This means that you can increase the load on a single server by increasing things like RAM, CPU or SSD. But on the other hand NoSQL databases are horizontally scalable. This means that you handle more traffic by sharding, or adding more servers in your NoSQL database. It is similar to adding more floors to the same building versus adding more buildings to the neighborhood. Thus NoSQL can ultimately become larger and more powerful, making these databases the preferred choice for large or ever-changing data sets.

4. The Structure –

SQL databases are table-based on the other hand NoSQL databases are either key-value pairs, document-based, graph databases or wide-column stores. This makes relational SQL databases a better option for applications that require multi-row transactions such as an accounting system or for legacy systems that were built for a relational structure.

5. Property followed –

SQL databases follow ACID properties (Atomicity, Consistency, Isolation and Durability) whereas the NoSQL database follows the Brewers CAP theorem (Consistency, Availability and Partition tolerance).

6. Support –

Great support is available for all SQL database from their vendors. Also a lot of independent consultations are there who can help you with SQL database for a very large scale deployments but for some NoSQL database you still have to rely on community support and only limited outside experts are available for setting up and deploying your large scale NoSQL deployments.

Some examples of SQL databases include PostgreSQL, MySQL, Oracle and Microsoft SQL Server. NoSQL database examples include Redis, RavenDB Cassandra, MongoDB, BigTable, HBase, Neo4j and CouchDB.

Textual ETL processing

ETL is a process in Data Warehousing and it stands for **Extract**, **Transform** and **Load**. It is a process in which an ETL tool extracts the data from various data source systems, transforms it in the staging area, and then finally, loads it into the Data Warehouse system.

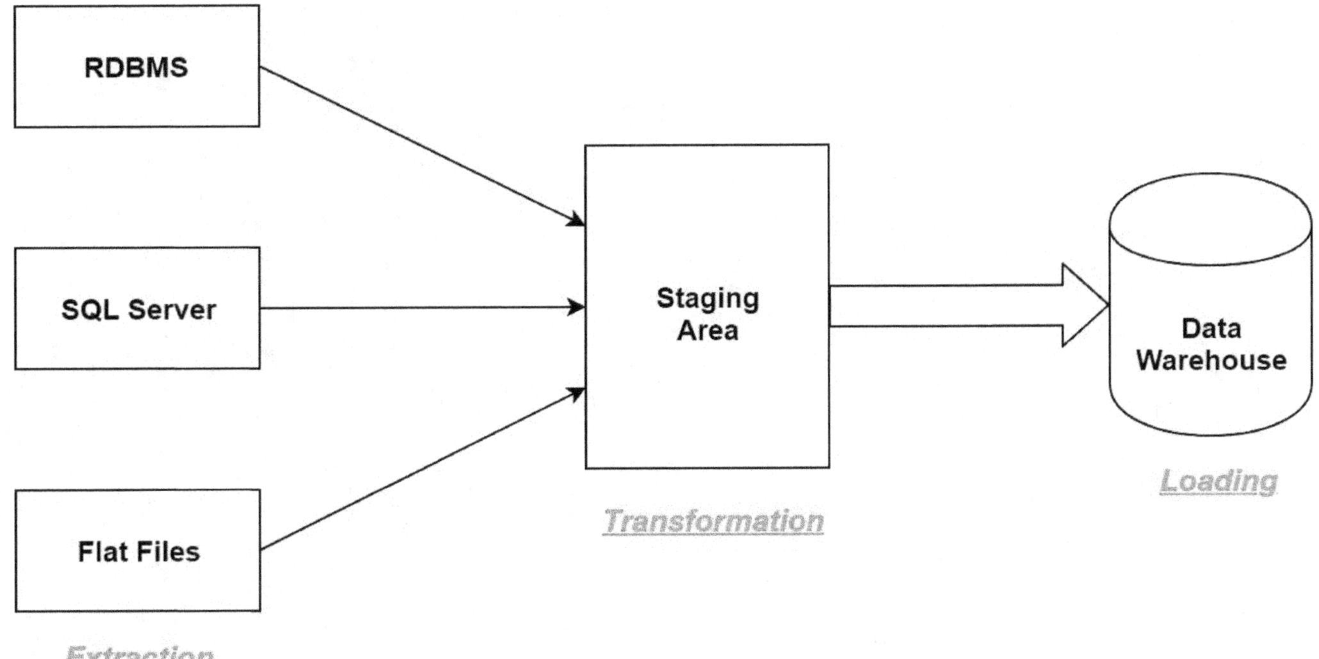

Let us understand each step of the ETL process in-depth:

Extraction:

The first step of the ETL process is extraction. In this step, data from various source systems is extracted which can be in various formats like relational databases, No SQL, XML, and flat files into the staging area. It is important to extract the data from various source systems and store it into the staging area first and not directly into the data warehouse because the extracted data is in various formats and can be corrupted also. Hence loading it directly into the data warehouse may damage it and rollback will be much more difficult. Therefore, this is one of the most important steps of ETL process.

Transformation:

The second step of the ETL process is transformation. In this step, a set of rules or functions are applied on the extracted data to convert it into a single standard format. It may involve following processes/tasks:

Filtering – loading only certain attributes into the data warehouse.

Cleaning – filling up the NULL values with some default values, mapping U.S.A, United States, and America into USA, etc.

Joining – joining multiple attributes into one.

Splitting – splitting a single attribute into multiple attributes.

Sorting – sorting tuples on the basis of some attribute (generally key-attribute)

Loading:

The third and final step of the ETL process is loading. In this step, the transformed data is finally loaded into the data warehouse. Sometimes the data is updated by loading into the data warehouse very frequently and sometimes it is done after longer but regular intervals. The rate and period of loading solely depends on the requirements and varies from system to system.

## CHAPTER FOUR

Big Data Analytics

Big data architectures

Big data architecture is the foundation for big data analytics. It is the overarching system used to manage large amounts of data so that it can be analyzed for business purposes, steer data analytics, and provide an environment in which big data analytics tools can extract vital business information from otherwise ambiguous data. The big data architecture framework serves as a reference blueprint for big data infrastructures and solutions, logically defining how big data solutions will work, the components that will be used, how information will flow, and security details.

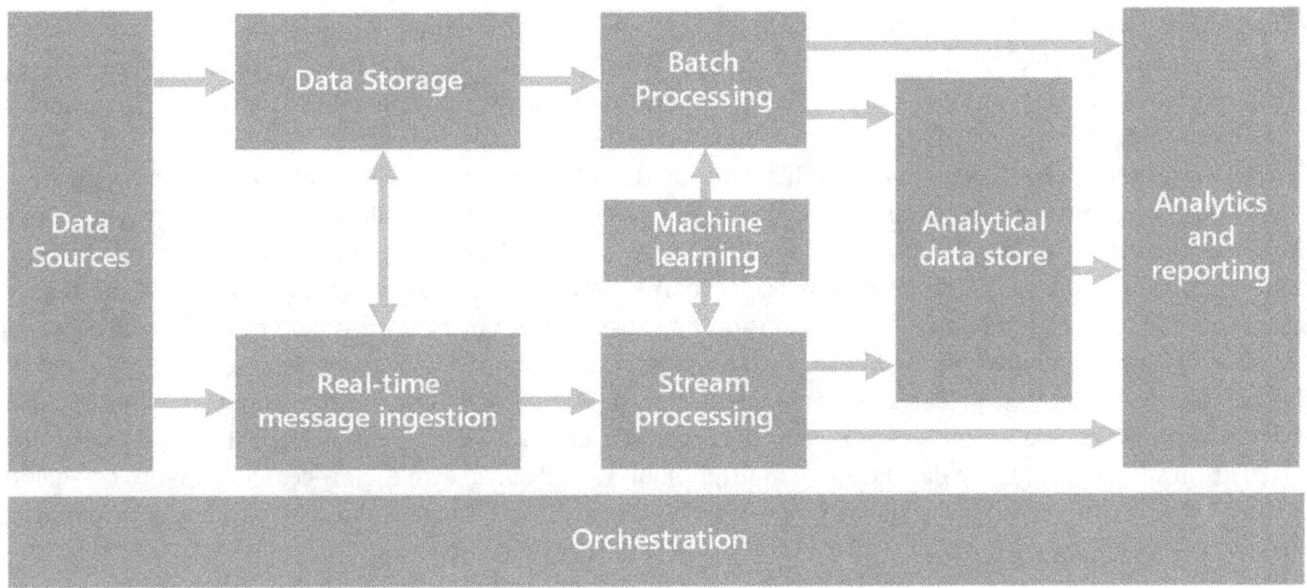

Fig. Big Data Architecture

Most big data architectures include some or all of the following components:
Data sources: All big data solutions start with one or more data sources. Examples include:

- Application data stores, such as relational databases.
- Static files produced by applications, such as web server log files.
- Real-time data sources, such as IoT devices.

Data storage: Data for batch processing operations is typically stored in a distributed file store that can hold high volumes of large files in various formats. This kind of store is often called a data lake. Options for implementing this storage include Azure Data Lake Store or blob containers in Azure Storage.

Batch processing: Because the data sets are so large, often a big data solution must process data files using long-running batch jobs to filter, aggregate, and otherwise prepare the data for analysis. Usually these jobs involve reading source files, processing them, and writing the output to new files. Options include running U-SQL jobs in Azure Data Lake Analytics, using Hive, Pig, or custom Map/Reduce jobs in an HDInsight Hadoop cluster, or using Java, Scala, or Python programs in an HDInsight Spark cluster.

Real-time message ingestion: If the solution includes real-time sources, the architecture must include a way to capture and store real-time messages for stream processing. This might be a simple data store, where incoming messages are dropped into a folder for processing. However, many solutions need a message ingestion store to act as a buffer for messages, and to support scale-out processing, reliable delivery, and other message queuing semantics. This portion of a streaming architecture is often referred to as stream buffering. Options include Azure Event Hubs, Azure IoT Hub, and Kafka.

Stream processing: After capturing real-time messages, the solution must process them by filtering, aggregating, and otherwise preparing the data for analysis. The processed stream data is then written to an output sink. Azure Stream Analytics provides a managed stream processing service based on perpetually running SQL queries that operate on unbounded streams. You can also use open source Apache streaming technologies like Storm and Spark Streaming in an HDInsight cluster.

Analytical data store: Many big data solutions prepare data for analysis and then serve the processed data in a structured format that can be queried using analytical tools. The analytical data store used to serve these queries can be a Kimball-style relational data warehouse, as seen in most traditional business intelligence (BI) solutions. Alternatively, the data could be presented through a low-latency NoSQL technology such as HBase, or an interactive Hive database that provides a metadata abstraction over data files in the distributed data store. Azure Synapse Analytics provides a managed service for large-scale, cloud-based data warehousing. HDInsight supports Interactive Hive, HBase, and Spark SQL, which can also be used to serve data for analysis.

Analysis and reporting: The goal of most big data solutions is to provide insights into the data through analysis and reporting. To empower users to analyze the data, the architecture may include a data modeling layer, such as a multidimensional OLAP cube or tabular data model in Azure Analysis Services. It might also support self-service BI, using the modeling and visualization technologies in Microsoft Power BI or Microsoft Excel. Analysis and reporting can also take the form of interactive data exploration by data scientists or data analysts. For these scenarios, many Azure services support analytical notebooks, such as Jupyter, enabling these users to leverage their existing skills with Python or R. For large-scale data exploration, you can use Microsoft R Server, either standalone or with Spark.

Orchestration: Most big data solutions consist of repeated data processing operations, encapsulated in workflows, that transform source data, move data between multiple sources and sinks, load the processed data into an analytical data store, or push the results straight to a report or dashboard. To automate these workflows, you can use an orchestration technology such Azure Data Factory or Apache Oozie and Sqoop.

Big Data Analytics Life Cycle

Big data analytics differs from traditional data analysis, mainly due to the fact that in big data, volume, variety, and velocity form the basis of data.

The Big Data Analytics Life cycle is divided into nine phases, named as :

1. Business Case/Problem Definition
2. Data Identification
3. Data Acquisition and filtration
4. Data Extraction
5. Data Munging(Validation and Cleaning)
6. Data Aggregation & Representation(Storage)
7. Exploratory Data Analysis

8. Data Visualization(Preparation for Modeling and Assessment)
9. Utilization of analysis results.

Let us discuss each phase:

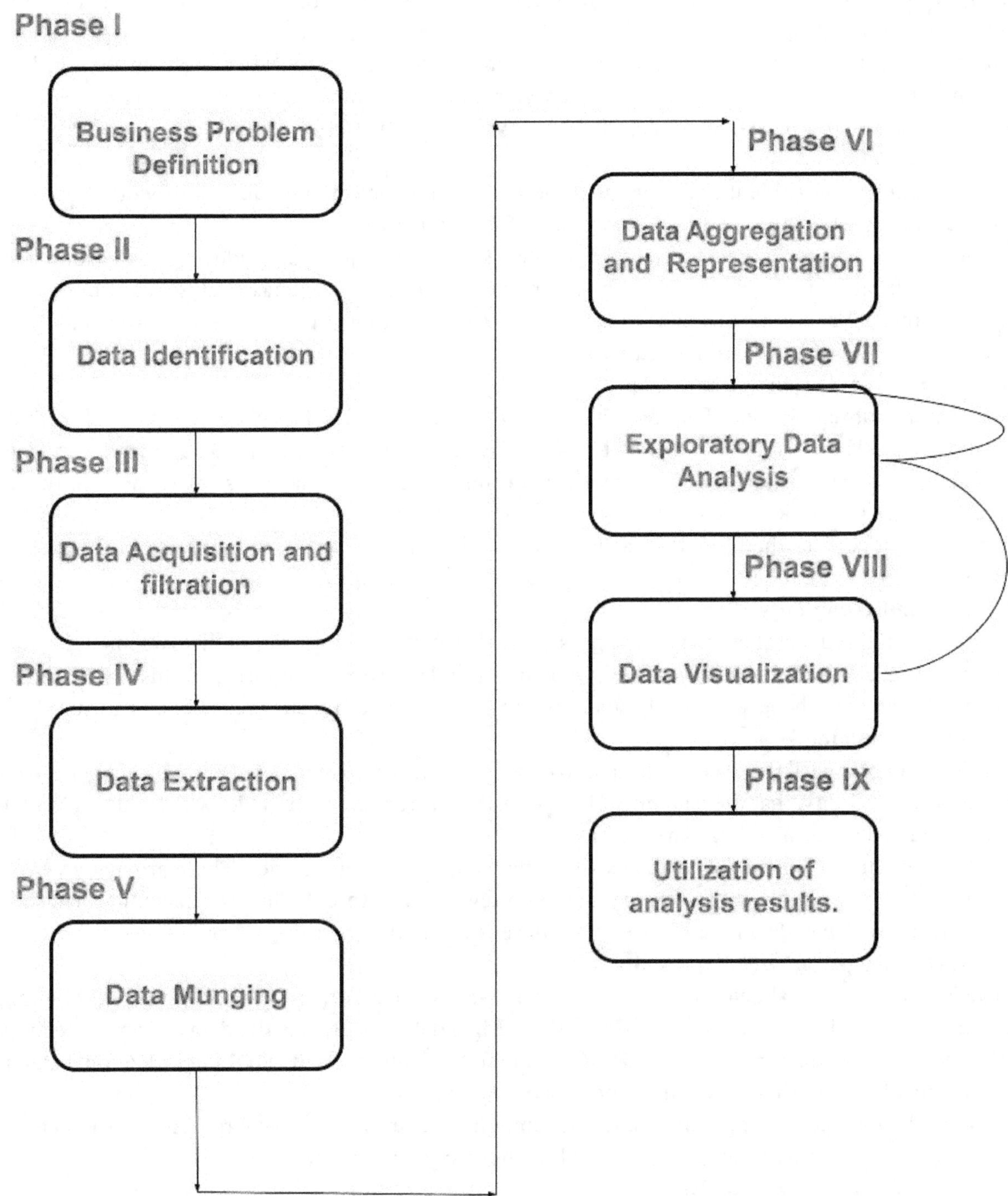

Fig. Big Data Analytics Life Cycle

Phase I-Business Problem Definition –

In this stage, the team learns about the business domain, which presents the motivation and goals for carrying out the analysis. In this stage, the problem is identified, and assumptions are made that how much potential gain a company will make after carrying out the analysis. Important activities in this step include framing the business problem as an analytics challenge that can be addressed in subsequent phases. It helps the decision-makers understand the business resources that will be required to be utilized thereby determining the underlying budget required to carry out the project.

Moreover, it can be determined, whether the problem identified, is a Big Data problem or not, based on the business requirements in the business case. To qualify as a big data problem, the business case should be directly related to one(or more) of the characteristics of volume, velocity, or variety.

Phase II- Data Definition –

Once the business case is identified, now it's time to find the appropriate datasets to work with. In this stage, analysis is done to see what other companies have done for a similar case.

Depending on the business case and the scope of analysis of the project being addressed, the sources of datasets can be either external or internal to the company. In the case of internal datasets, the datasets can include data collected from internal sources, such as feedback forms, from existing software, On the other hand, for external datasets, the list includes datasets from third-party providers.

Phase III- Data Acquisition and filtration –

Once the source of data is identified, now it is time to gather the data from such sources. This kind of data is mostly unstructured. Then it is subjected to filtration, such as removal of the corrupt data or irrelevant data, which is of no scope to the analysis objective. Here corrupt data means data that may have missing records, or the ones, which include incompatible data types.

After filtration, a copy of the filtered data is stored and compressed, as it can be of use in the future, for some other analysis.

Phase IV- Data Extraction –

Now the data is filtered, but there might be a possibility that some of the entries of the data might be incompatible, to rectify this issue, a separate phase is created, known as the data extraction phase. In this phase, the data, which don't match with the underlying scope of the analysis, are extracted and transformed in such a form.

Phase V- Data Munging –

As mentioned in phase III, the data is collected from various sources, which results in the data being unstructured. There might be a possibility, that the data might have constraints, that are unsuitable, which can lead to false results. Hence there is a need to clean and validate the data.

It includes removing any invalid data and establishing complex validation rules. There are many ways to validate and clean the data. For example, a dataset might contain few rows, with null entries. If a similar dataset is present, then those entries are copied from that dataset, else those rows are dropped.

Phase VI- Data Aggregation & Representation –

The data is cleansed and validates, against certain rules set by the enterprise. But the data might be spread across multiple datasets, and it is not advisable to work with multiple datasets. Hence, the datasets are joined together. For example: If there are two datasets, namely that of a Student Academic section and Student Personal Details section, then both can be joined together via common fields, i.e. roll number.

This phase calls for intensive operation since the amount of data can be very large. Automation can be brought into consideration, so that these things are executed, without any human intervention.

Phase VII- Exploratory Data Analysis –

Here comes the actual step, the analysis task. Depending on the nature of the big data problem, analysis is carried out. Data analysis can be classified as Confirmatory analysis and Exploratory analysis. In confirmatory analysis, the cause of a phenomenon is analyzed before. The assumption is called the hypothesis. The data is analyzed to approve or disapprove the hypothesis.

This kind of analysis provides definitive answers to some specific questions and confirms whether an assumption was true or not.In an exploratory analysis, the data is explored to obtain information, why a phenomenon occurred. This type of analysis answers "why" a phenomenon occurred. This kind of analysis doesn't provide definitive, meanwhile, it provides discovery of patterns.

Phase VIII- Data Visualization –

Now we have the answer to some questions, using the information from the data in the datasets. But these answers are still in a form that can't be presented to business users. A sort of representation is required to obtains value or some conclusion from the analysis. Hence, various tools are used to visualize the data in graphic form, which can easily be interpreted by business users.

Visualization is said to influence the interpretation of the results. Moreover, it allows the users to discover answers to questions that are yet to be formulated.

Phase IX- Utilization of analysis results –

The analysis is done, the results are visualized, now it's time for the business users to make decisions to utilize the results. The results can be used for optimization, to refine the business process. It can also be used as an input for the systems to enhance performance.

Data Analytics and its type

Analytics is the discovery and communication of meaningful patterns in data. Especially, valuable in areas rich with recorded information, analytics relies on the simultaneous application of statistics, computer programming, and operation research to qualify performance. Analytics often favors data visualization to communicate insight.

Firms may commonly apply analytics to business data, to describe, predict, and improve business performance. Especially, areas within include predictive analytics, enterprise decision management, etc. Since analytics can require extensive computation(because of big data), the algorithms and software used to analytics harness the most current methods in computer science.

There are four types of data analytics:

1. Predictive (forecasting)
2. Descriptive (business intelligence and data mining)
3. Prescriptive (optimization and simulation)
4. Diagnostic analytics

Predictive Analytics: Predictive analytics turn the data into valuable, actionable information. predictive analytics uses data to determine the probable outcome of an event or a likelihood of a situation occurring.

Predictive analytics holds a variety of statistical techniques from modeling, machine, learning, data mining, and game theory that analyze current and historical facts to make predictions about a future event. Techniques that are used for predictive analytics are:

- Linear Regression
- Time series analysis and forecasting
- Data Mining

Descriptive Analytics: Descriptive analytics looks at data and analyze past event for insight as to how to approach future events. It looks at the past performance and understands the performance by mining historical data to understand the cause of success or failure in the past. Almost all management reporting such as sales, marketing, operations, and finance uses this type of analysis.

The descriptive model quantifies relationships in data in a way that is often used to classify customers or prospects into groups. Unlike a predictive model that focuses on predicting the behavior of a single customer, Descriptive analytics identifies many different relationships between customer and product.

Common examples of Descriptive analytics are company reports that provide historic reviews like:

- Data Queries
- Reports
- Descriptive Statistics
- Data dashboard

Prescriptive Analytics: Prescriptive Analytics automatically synthesize big data, mathematical science, business rule, and machine learning to make a prediction and then suggests a decision option to take advantage of the prediction.

Prescriptive analytics goes beyond predicting future outcomes by also suggesting action benefit from the predictions and showing the decision maker the implication of each decision option. Prescriptive Analytics not only anticipates what will happen and when to happen but also why it will happen. Further, Prescriptive Analytics can suggest decision options on how to take advantage of a future opportunity or mitigate a future risk and illustrate the implication of each decision option.

For example, Prescriptive Analytics can benefit healthcare strategic planning by using analytics to leverage operational and usage data combined with data of external factors such as economic data, population demography, etc.

Diagnostic Analytics: In this analysis, we generally use historical data over other data to answer any question or for the solution of any problem. We try to find any dependency and pattern in the historical data of the particular problem.

For example, companies go for this analysis because it gives a great insight into a problem, and they also keep detailed information about their disposal otherwise data collection may turn out individual for every problem and it will be very time-consuming. Common techniques used for Diagnostic Analytics are:

- Data discovery
- Data mining
- Correlations

Analytical Approaches:

1. Data fusion and data integration:

By combining a set of techniques that analyze and integrate data from multiple sources and solutions, the insights are more efficient and potentially more accurate than if developed through a single source of data.

1. Data mining:

A common tool used within big data analytics, data mining extracts patterns from large data sets by combining methods from statistics and machine learning, within database management. An example would be when customer data is mined to determine which segments are most likely to react to an offer.

3. Machine learning:

Well known within the field of artificial intelligence, machine learning is also used for data analysis. Emerging from computer science, it works with computer algorithms to produce assumptions based on data. It provides predictions that would be impossible for human analysts.

4. Natural language processing (NLP):

Known as a subspecialty of computer science, artificial intelligence, and linguistics, this data analysis tool uses algorithms to analyze human (natural) language.

5. Statistics:

This technique works to collect, organize, and interpret data, within surveys and experiments. Other data analysis techniques include spatial analysis, predictive modelling, association rule learning, network analysis and many, many more. The technologies that process, manage, and analyze this data are of an entirely different and expansive field, that similarly evolves and develops over time. Techniques and technologies aside, any form or size of data is valuable. Managed accurately and effectively, it can reveal a host of business, product, and market insights. What does the future of data analysis look like? It's hard to say with the tremendous pace analytics and technology progresses, but undoubtedly data innovation is changing the face of business and society in its holistic entirety.

Data Analytics with Mathematical manipulations

Data Manipulation- Manipulation of data is the process of manipulating or changing information to make it more organized and readable. We use DML to accomplish this. What is meant by DML? Well, it stands for Data Manipulation Language or a programming language capable of adding, removing, and altering databases, i.e. changing the information to something that we can read. We can clean and map the data thanks to DML to make it digestible for expression.

Data Manipulation is the modification of information to make it easier to read or more structured. For example, in alphabetical order, a log of data may be sorted, making it easier to find individual entries. On web server logs, data manipulation is also used to allow the website owner to monitor their most famous pages and their sources of traffic.

For business operations and optimization, data manipulation is a key feature. You have to be able to deal with the data in the way you need it to use data properly and turn it into valuable information such as analyzing financial data, consumer behavior, and doing trend analysis. As such, data manipulation provides an organization with many advantages, including:

- Consistent data: It can be structured, read, and better understood by providing data in a consistent format. You may not have a unified view when taking data from various sources, but with data manipulation and commands, you can make sure that the data is structured and stored consistently.
- Project data: it is paramount for organizations to be able to use historical data to project the future and to provide more in-depth analysis, especially when it comes to finances. Manipulation of data makes it possible for this purpose.
- Overall, being able to convert, update, delete, and incorporate data into a database means you can do more with the data. -Create more value from the data. It becomes pointless by providing data that remains static. But you will have straightforward insights to make better business decisions when you know how to use data to your advantage.
- Delete or neglect redundant data: data that is unusable is always present and can interfere with what matters.

IN EXCEL, HOW DO YOU MANIPULATE DATA?

Manipulation of data in Python and manipulation of data in R are critical aspects of data manipulation. Before moving through the more profound principles of Data Manipulation in Python and R, let us now understand how to manipulate data.

Most definitely, you are aware of how to use MS Excel. Here are some tips to help you manipulate Excel info.

- **Formulas and functions** – Addition, subtraction, multiplication, and division are some of the basic math functions in Excel. You need to know how to use these Excel-critical features.
- **Autofill in Excel**-When you want to use the same equation across several cells, this feature is useful. One way of doing it is to retype the formula. Another way is to drag the cursor to the cell's lower right corner and then downwards. It will help you simultaneously apply the same formula to several rows.
- **Sort and Filter**- Users can save a lot of time when analyzing data by sorting and filtering options in Excel.
- **Removing duplicates**-There are often chances of replication of data in the process of collecting and assimilating data. In Excel, the Delete Duplicate feature can help remove duplicate spreadsheet entries.
- **Column splitting, merging, and merging**-Columns or rows in Excel may often be added or removed. Data organization often requires integrating, splitting, or combining multiple datasheets.

Data Ingestion

Data Ingestion is the process of, transferring data, from varied sources to an approach, where it can be analyzed, archived, or utilized by an establishment. The usual steps, involved in this process, are drawing out data, from its current place, converting the data, and, finally loading it, in a location, for efficient research.

Data ingestion helps teams go fast. The scope of any given data pipeline is deliberately narrow, giving data teams flexibility and agility at scale. Once parameters are set, data analysts and data scientists can easily build a single data pipeline to move data to their system of choice. Common examples of data ingestion include:

- Move data from Salesforce.com to a data warehouse then analyze with Tableau
- Capture data from a Twitter feed for real-time sentiment analysis
- Acquire data for training machine learning models and experimentation

we will be converting, data present in the following files, to dataframe structures –

- Read data from CSV file
- Read data from Excel file
- Read data from JSON file
- Read data from Clipboard
- Read data from HTML table from web page
- Read data from SQLite table

Read data from CSV file

To load, data present in Comma-separated file(CSV), we will follow steps as below:

- Prepare your sample dataset. Here, we have a CSV file, containing information, about Indian Metro cities. It describes if the city is a Tier1 or Tier2 city, their geographical location, state they belong to, and if it is a coastal city.
- Use Pandas method 'read_csv'
- Method used – read_csv(file_path)
- Parameter – String format, containing the path of the file and its name, or, URL when present on the remote server. It reads, the file data, and, converts it, into a valid two-dimensional dataframe object. This method can be used to read data, present in ".csv" as well as ".txt" file formats.

The code to get the data in a Pandas Data Frame is:
Import the Pandas library

import pandas
# Load data from Comma separated file
# Use method - read_csv(filepath)
# Parameter - the path/URL of the CSV/TXT file
dfIndianMetros = pandas.read_csv("gfg_indianmetros.csv")
# print the dataframe object
print(dfIndianMetros)
Output:

```
# print the dataframe object
print(dfIndianMetros)
```

```
          NAME           STATE    LAT    LON SEA  Tier
0    NEW DELHI           DELHI  28.65  77.23   N     1
1       MUMBAI     MAHARASHTRA  19.07  72.88   Y     1
2      CHENNAI      TAMIL NADU  13.08  80.27   Y     1
3      KOLKATA     WEST BENGAL  22.56  88.36   Y     1
4    AHMEDABAD         GUJARAT  23.02  72.58   N     1
5        PATNA           BIHAR  25.59  85.13   N     2
6       KANPUR   UTTAR PRADESH  26.46  80.34   N     2
7       BHOPAL  MADHYA PRADESH  23.25  77.40   N     2
8         PUNE     MAHARASHTRA  18.51  73.85   N     1
9    HYDERABAD       TELANGANA  17.38  78.45   N     1
10      JAIPUR       RAJASTHAN  26.91  75.78   N     2
11       SURAT         GUJARAT  23.02  72.58   Y     2
12   BENGALURU       KARNATAKA  12.97  77.59   N     1
13 BHUVANESHWAR         ODISSA  20.29  85.82   Y     2
14      RANCHI       JHARKHAND  23.34  85.30   N     2
15      COCHIN          KERALA   9.93  76.26   Y     2
```

Read data from an Excel file

To load data present in an Excel file(.xlsx, .xls) we will follow steps as below-

- Prepare your sample dataset. Here, we have an Excel file, containing information about Bakery and its branches. It describes the number of employees, address of branches of the bakery.
- Use Pandas method 'read_excel' .
- Method used – read_excel(file_path)
- Parameter – The method accepts, the path of the file and its name, in string format as a parameter. The file can be on a remote server, or, on a machine locally. It reads the file data, and, converts it, into a valid two-dimensional data frame object. This method, can be used, to read data present in ".xlsx" as well as ".xls" file formats.

The file contents are as follows:

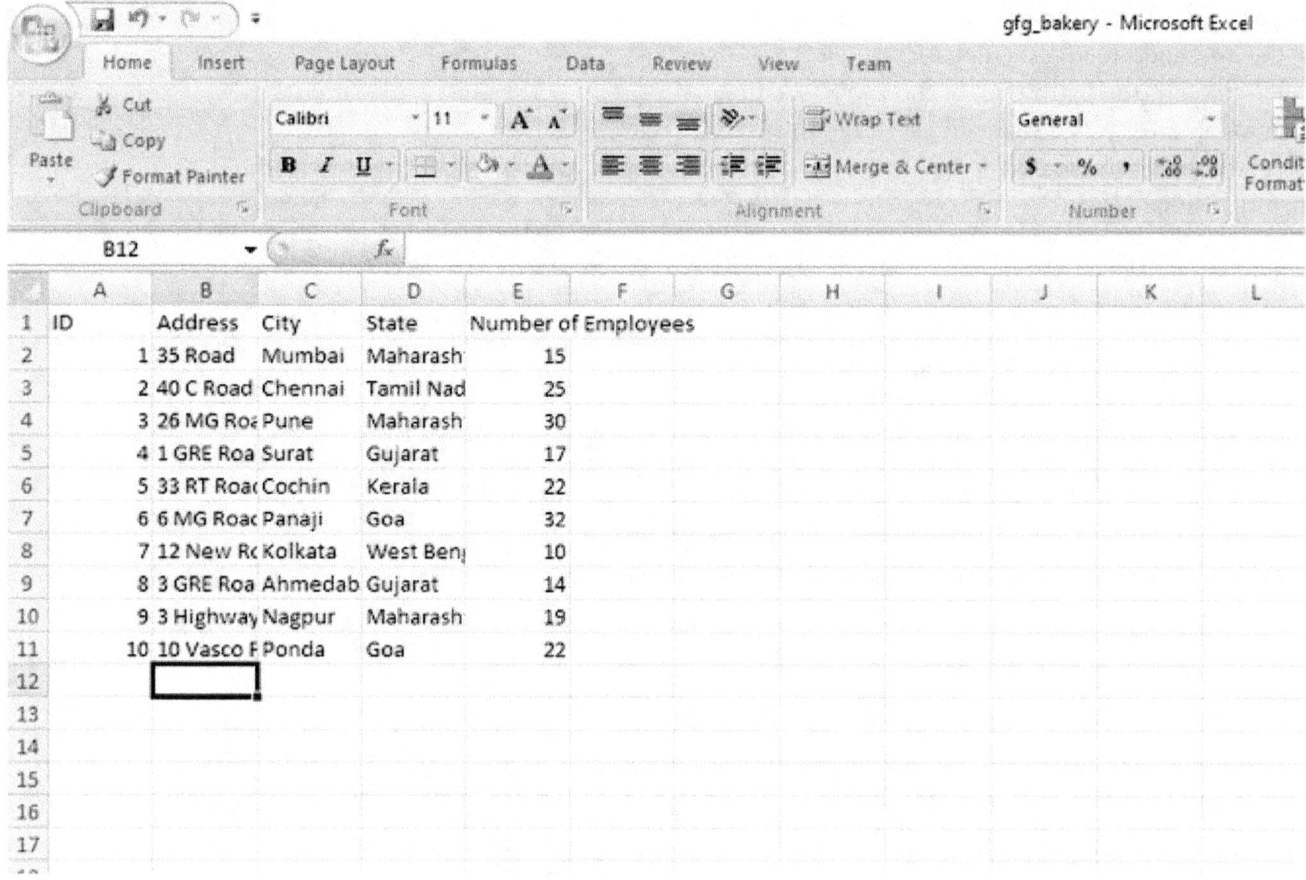

The code to get the data in a Pandas DataFrame is:

```
# Import the Pandas library
import pandas
# Load data from an Excel file
# Use method - read_excel(filepath)
# Method parameter - The file location(URL/path) and name
dfBakery = pandas.read_excel("gfg_bakery.xlsx")
# print the dataframe object
print(dfBakery)
```

```python
# print the dataframe object
print(dfBakery)
```

```
   ID       Address        City          State  Number of Employees
0   1       35 Road      Mumbai    Maharashtra                   15
1   2      40 C Road     Chennai     Tamil Nadu                   25
2   3     26 MG Road        Pune    Maharashtra                   30
3   4     1 GRE Road       Surat        Gujarat                   17
4   5     33 RT Road      Cochin         Kerala                   22
5   6      6 MG Road      Panaji            Goa                   32
6   7    12 New Road     Kolkata    West Bengal                   10
7   8     3 GRE Road   Ahmedabad        Gujarat                   14
8   9     3 Highway      Nagpur    Maharashtra                   19
9  10  10 Vasco Road       Ponda            Goa                   22
```

Read data from a JSON file

To load data present in a JavaScript Object Notation file(.json) we will follow steps as below:

- Prepare your sample dataset. Here, we have a JSON file, containing information about Countries and their dial code.
- Use Pandas method 'read_json'.
- Method used – read_json(file_path)
- Parameter – This method, accepts the path of the file and its name, in string format, as a parameter. It reads the file data, and, converts it, into a valid two-dimensional data frame object.

The file contents are as follows:

```
E:\TeachPytho\Charm_HeloWorld\gfg_codecountry.json - Notepad++
File  Edit  Search  View  Encoding  Language  Settings  Tools  Macro  Run  Plugins  Window  ?

gfg_codecountry.json
 1  [{"name":"Israel","dial_code":"+972","code":"IL"},
 2  {"name":"Australia","dial_code":"+61","code":"AU"},
 3  {"name":"Austria","dial_code":"+43","code":"AT"},
 4  {"name":"Belgium","dial_code":"+32","code":"BE"},
 5  {"name":"Botswana","dial_code":"+267","code":"BW"},
 6  {"name":"Brazil","dial_code":"+55","code":"BR"},
 7  {"name":"Greece","dial_code":"+30","code":"GR"},
 8  {"name":"Greenland","dial_code":"+299","code":"GL"},
 9  {"name":"Grenada","dial_code":"+1 473","code":"GD"},
10  {"name":"Guadeloupe","dial_code":"+590","code":"GP"},
11  {"name":"Guam","dial_code":"+1 671","code":"GU"},
12  {"name":"Guyana","dial_code":"+595","code":"GY"},
13  {"name":"Haiti","dial_code":"+509","code":"HT"}]
```

The code to get the data in a Pandas DataFrame is:

```python
# Import the Pandas library
import pandas
# Load data from a JSON file
# Use method - read_json(filepath)
# Method parameter - The file location(URL/path) and name
dfCodeCountry = pandas.read_json("gfg_codecountry.json")
# print the dataframe object
print(dfCodeCountry)
```

```
# print the dataframe object
print(dfCodeCountry)
```

```
    code dial_code        name
0     IL      +972      Israel
1     AU       +61   Australia
2     AT       +43     Austria
3     BE       +32     Belgium
4     BW      +267    Botswana
5     BR       +55      Brazil
6     GR       +30      Greece
7     GL      +299   Greenland
8     GD    +1 473     Grenada
9     GP      +590  Guadeloupe
10    GU    +1 671        Guam
11    GY      +595      Guyana
12    HT      +509       Haiti
```

Read data from Clipboard

We can also transfer data present in Clipboard to a dataframe object. A clipboard is a part of Random Access Memory(RAM), where copied data is present. Whenever we copy any file, text, image, or any type of data, using the 'Copy' command, it gets stored in the Clipboard. To convert, data present here, follow the steps as mentioned below –

- Select all the contents of the file. The file should be a CSV file. It can be a '.txt' file as well, containing comma-separated values, as shown in the example. Please note, if the file contents are not in a favorable format, then, one can get a Parser Error at runtime.
- Right, Click and say Copy. Now, this data is transferred, to the computer Clipboard.
- Use Pandas method 'read_clipboard' .
- Method used – read_clipboard
- Parameter – The method, does not accept any parameter. It reads the latest copied data as present in the clipboard, and, converts it, into a valid two-dimensional dataframe object.

The file contents selected are as follows:

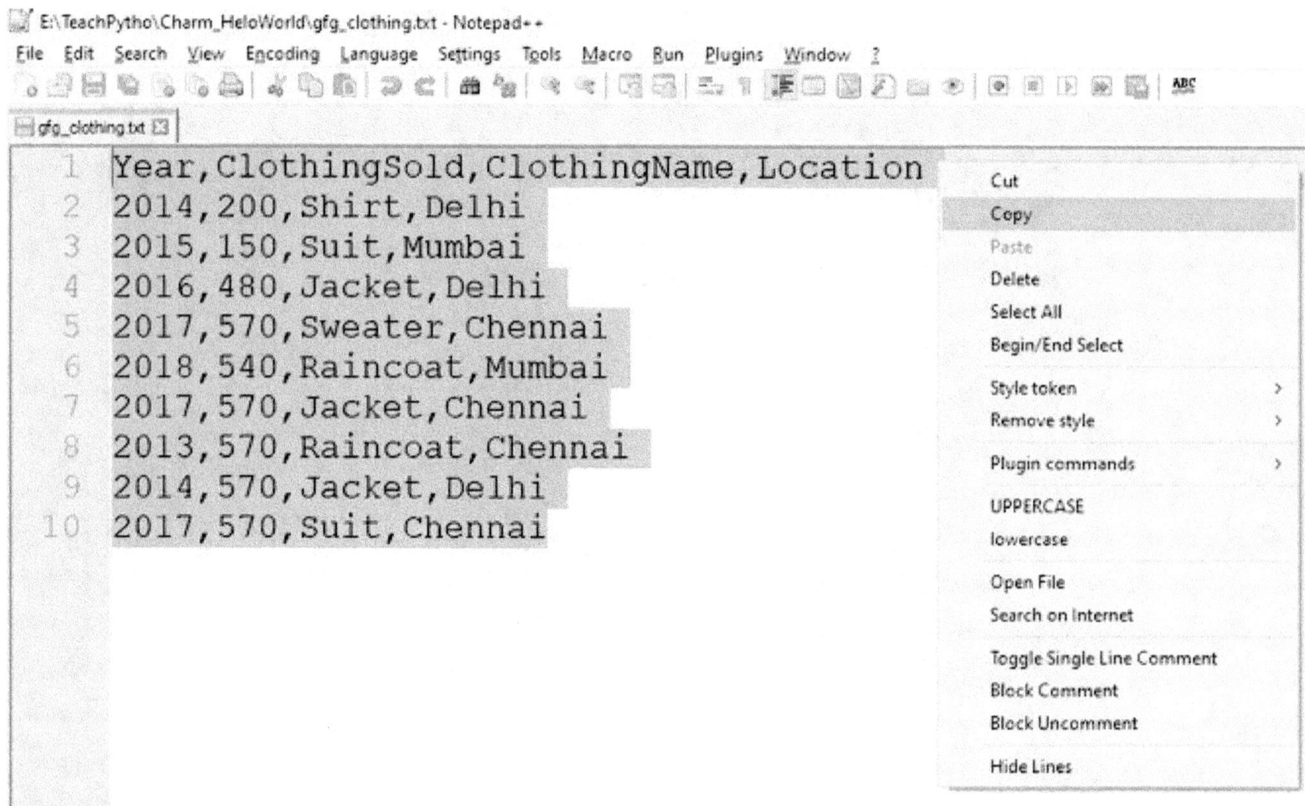

The code to get the data in a Pandas DataFrame is:
# Import the required library
import pandas
# Copy file contents which are in proper format
# Whatever data you have copied will
# get transferred to dataframe object
# Method does not accept any parameter
pdCopiedData = pd.read_clipboard()
# Print the data frame object
print(pdCopiedData)

```
#Print the dataframe object
print(pdCopiedData)

   Year,ClothingSold,ClothingName,Location
0                 2014,200,Shirt,Delhi
1                 2015,150,Suit,Mumbai
2                 2016,480,Jacket,Delhi
3               2017,570,Sweater,Chennai
4              2018,540,Raincoat,Mumbai
5                2017,570,Jacket,Chennai
6              2013,570,Raincoat,Chennai
7                 2014,570,Jacket,Delhi
8                2017,570,Suit,Chennai
```

Read data from HTML file

A webpage is usually made of HTML elements. There are different HTML tags such as <head>, <title> , <table>, <div> based on the purpose of data display, on browser. We can transfer, the content between <table> element, present in an HTML webpage, to a Pandas data frame object. Follow the steps as mentioned below –

- Select all the elements present in the <table>, between start and end tags. Assign it, to a Python variable.
- Use Pandas method 'read_html' .
- Method used – read_html(string within <table> tag)
- Parameter – The method, accepts string variable, containing the elements present between <table> tag. It reads the elements, traversing through the table, <tr> and <td> tags, and, converts it, into a list object. The first element of the list object is the desired dataframe object.

Write the following code to convert the HTML table content in the Pandas Dataframe object:

```
# Import the Pandas library
import pandas
# Variable containing the elements
# between <table> tag from webpage
html_string = """
<table>
<thead>
<tr>
<th>Date</th>
<th>Empname</th>
<th>Year</th>
<th>Rating</th>
<th>Region</th>
</tr>
</thead>
<tbody>
<tr>
```

```
<td>2020-01-01</td>
<td>Savio</td>
<td>2004</td>
<td>0.5</td>
<td>South</td>
</tr>
<tr>
<td>2020-01-02</td>
<td>Rahul</td>
<td>1998</td>
<td>1.34</td>
<td>East</td>
</tr>
<tr>
<td>2020-01-03</td>
<td>Tina</td>
<td>1988</td>
<td>1.00023</td>
<td>West</td>
</tr>
<tr>
<td>2021-01-03</td>
<td>Sonia</td>
<td>2001</td>
<td>2.23</td>
<td>North</td>
</tr>
<tr>
<td>2008-01-03</td>
<td>Milo</td>
<td>2008</td>
<td>3.23</td>
<td>East</td>
</tr>
<tr>
<td>2006-01-03</td>
<td>Edward</td>
<td>2005</td>
<td>0.43</td>
<td>West</td>
</tr>
</tbody>
</table>"""
# Pass the string containing html table element
df = pandas.read_html(html_string)
# Since read_html, returns a list object,
# extract first element of the list
dfHtml = df[0]
```

# Print the data frame object
print(dfHtml)

```
#Print the data frame object
print(dfHtml)
```

```
         Date Empname  Year   Rating Region
0  2020-01-01   Savio  2004  0.50000  South
1  2020-01-02   Rahul  1998  1.34000   East
2  2020-01-03    Tina  1988  1.00023   West
3  2021-01-03   Sonia  2001  2.23000  North
4  2008-01-03    Milo  2008  3.23000   East
5  2006-01-03  Edward  2005  0.43000   West
```

Read data from SQL table

We can convert, data present in database tables, to valid dataframe objects as well. Python allows easy interface, with a variety of databases, such as SQLite, MySQL, MongoDB, etc. SQLite is a lightweight database, which can be embedded in any program. The SQLite database holds all the related SQL tables. We can load, SQLite table data, to a Pandas dataframe object. Follow the steps, as mentioned below –

- Prepare a sample SQLite table using 'DB Browser for SQLite tool' or any such tool. These tools allow the effortless creation, edition of database files compatible with SQLite. The database file, has a '.db' file extension. In this example, we have 'Novels.db' file, containing a table called "novels". This table has information about Novels, such as Novel Name, Price, Genre, etc.
- Here, to connect to the database, we will import the 'sqlite3' module, in our code. The sqlite3 module, is an interface, to connect to the SQLite databases. The sqlite3 library is included in Python, since Python version 2.5. Hence, no separate installation is required. To connect to the database, we will use the SQLite method 'connect', which returns a connection object. The connect method accepts the following parameters:

- database_name – The name of the database in which the table is present. This is a .db extension file. If the file is present, an open connection object is returned. If the file is not present, it is created first and then a connection object is returned.
- Use Pandas method 'read_sql_query'.
- Method used – read_sql_query
- Parameter – This method accepts the following parameters
- SQL query – Select query, to fetch the required rows from the table.
- Connection object – The connection object returned by the 'connect' method. The read_sql_query method, converts, the resultant rows of the query, to a dataframe object.
- Print the dataframe object using the print method.

# Import the required libraries
import sqlite3
import pandas
# Prepare a connection object

```
# Pass the Database name as a parameter
conn = sqlite3.connect("Novels.db")
# Use read_sql_query method
# Pass SELECT query and connection object as parameter
pdSql = pd.read_sql_query("SELECT * FROM novels", conn)
# Print the dataframe object
print(pdSql)
# Close the connection object
conn.close()
```

```
#Print the dataframe object
print(pdSql)
```

	novelName	author	genre	noOfPrints	price
0	Crooked Tree	Agatha Christie	Mystery	12	300.0
1	SecretSeven	Enid Blyton	Adventure	34	230.0
2	Famous Five	Enid Blyton	Adventure	23	150.0
3	Harry Potter	JK Rowling	Fantasy	30	250.0
4	Malory Towers	Enid Blyton	Adventure	35	300.0

Data Cleaning:

As a data scientist, one of the biggest struggles is cleansing the data before one can actually dive into it to get some meaningful insights. Data cleaning is one of the most important steps which should never be ignored. If the data is not cleaned thoroughly, the accuracy of your model stands on shaky grounds

Poor quality of data leads to biased results with low accuracy high error percentages thus, it is important to clean the data thoroughly before fitting a model to it. As a data scientist, it is important to understand that all the data provided to us may not be useful and hence we must know the ways to treat them.

What is data cleaning – Removing null records, dropping unnecessary columns, treating missing values, rectifying junk values or otherwise called outliers, restructuring the data to modify it to a more readable format, etc is known as data cleaning.

Data cleaning is not just erasing the existing information to add the new information, but rather finding a way to maximize a data set's accuracy without necessarily losing the existing information. Different types of data will require different types of cleaning, but always remember that the correct approach is the deciding factor.

After cleansing the data, it will become consistent with other similar data sets in the system. Let's look at the steps for cleaning the data.

One of the most common data cleaning examples is its application in data warehouses. A data warehouse stores a variety of data from numerous sources and optimizes it for analysis before any model fitting can be done.

Removing Null/Duplicate Records

If in a particular row a significant amount of data is missing, then it would be better to drop that row as it would not be adding any value to our model. you can impute the value; provide an appropriate substitute for the missing data. Also always remember to delete duplicate/ redundant values from your dataset as they might result in a bias in your model.

For example, let us consider the student dataset with the following records.

name score address height weight

A 56 Goa 165 56

B 45 Mumbai 130 65

C 87 Delhi 170 58

D

E 99 Mysore 167 60

As we see that corresponding to student name "D", most of the data is missing hence we drop that particular row.

student_df.dropna() # drops rows with 1 or more Nan value

#output

name score address height weight

A 56 Goa 165 56

B 45 Mumbai 130 65

C 87 Delhi 170 58

E 99 Mysore 167 60

Dropping unnecessary Columns

When we receive the data from stakeholders, generally it is huge. There can be a log of data that might not add any value to our model. Such data is better removed as it would valuable resources like memory and processing time.

For example, while looking at students' performance over a test, students' weight or their height does not have anything to contribute to the model.

student_df.drop(['height','weight'], axis = 1,inplace=True) #Drops Height column form the dataframe

#output

name score address

A 56 Goa

B 45 Mumbai

C 87 Delhi

E 99 Mysore

Some data cleansing tools

- Openrefine
- Trifacta Wrangler
- TIBCO Clarity
- Cloudingo
- IBM Infosphere Quality Stage

Data Imputation

Imputation is a technique used for replacing the missing data with some substitute value to retain most of the data/ information of the dataset. These techniques are used because removing the data from the dataset every time is not feasible and can lead to a reduction in the size of the dataset to a large extend, which not only raises concerns for biasing the dataset but also leads to incorrect analysis.

Imputation Techniques

Fig. Data Impulsion Technique

1. Complete Case Analysis(CCA):-

This is a quite straightforward method of handling the Missing Data, which directly removes the rows that have missing data i.e we consider only those rows where we have complete data i.e data is not missing. This method is also popularly known as "Listwise deletion".

Assumptions:-

- Data is Missing At Random(MAR).
- Missing data is completely removed from the table.

Advantages:-

- Easy to implement.
- No Data manipulation required.

Limitations:-

- Deleted data can be informative.
- Can lead to the deletion of a large part of the data.
- Can create a bias in the dataset, if a large amount of a particular type of variable is deleted from it.
- The production model will not know what to do with Missing data.

When to Use:-

- Data is MAR(Missing At Random).
- Good for Mixed, Numerical, and Categorical data.
- Missing data is not more than 5% – 6% of the dataset.
- Data doesn't contain much information and will not bias the dataset.

2. Arbitrary Value Imputation

This is an important technique used in Imputation as it can handle both the Numerical and Categorical variables. This technique states that we group the missing values in a column and assign them to a new value that is far away from the range of that column. Mostly we use values like 99999999 or -9999999 or "Missing" or "Not defined" for numerical & categorical variables.

Assumptions:-

- Data is not Missing At Random.
- The missing data is imputed with an arbitrary value that is not part of the dataset or Mean/Median/Mode of data.

Advantages:-

- Easy to implement.
- We can use it in production.
- It retains the importance of "missing values" if it exists.

Disadvantages:-

- Can distort original variable distribution.
- Arbitrary values can create outliers.
- Extra caution required in selecting the Arbitrary value.

When to Use:-

- When data is not MAR(Missing At Random).
- Suitable for All.

3. Frequent Category Imputation

This technique says to replace the missing value with the variable with the highest frequency or in simple words replacing the values with the Mode of that column. This technique is also referred to as Mode Imputation.

Assumptions:-

- Data is missing at random.
- There is a high probability that the missing data looks like the majority of the data.

Advantages:-

- Implementation is easy.
- We can obtain a complete dataset in very little time.
- We can use this technique in the production model.

Disadvantages:-

- The higher the percentage of missing values, the higher will be the distortion.
- May lead to over-representation of a particular category.
- Can distort original variable distribution.

When to Use:-

- Data is Missing at Random(MAR)
- Missing data is not more than 5% – 6% of the dataset.

Data standardization

Data standardization is the process of converting data to a common format to enable users to process and analyze it. Most organizations utilize data from a number of sources; this can include data warehouses, lakes, cloud storage, and databases. However, data from disparate sources can be problematic if it isn't uniform, leading to difficulties down the line.

Getting there involves converting that data into a uniform format, with logical and consistent definitions. These definitions will form your metadata — the labels that identify the what, how, why, who, when, and where of your data. That's the basis of your data standardization process.

Data Standardization enables the data consumer to analyze and use data in a consistent manner. Typically, when data is created and stored in the source system, it's structured in a particular way that is often unknown to the data consumer. Moreover, datasets that might be semantically related may be stored and represented differently, thereby making it difficult for a data consumer to aggregate or compare the datasets.

Data Standardization Use Cases

There are two main use case categories in Data Standardization: Source-to-Target Mapping, and Complex Reconciliation. We typically divide the former into two sub-categories thereby arriving at three use cases:

- Simple mapping from external sources: This use case handles on-boarding data from systems that are external to the organization, and mapping its keys and values to an output schema.
- Simple mapping from internal sources: This use case involves handling internal datasets that are based on inconsistent definitions and transforming them into a single trustworthy data set for the entire organization.
- Complex reconciliation: This use case involves the creation of complex calculated metrics that provide their own semantics based on defined business logic.

Data Standardization Examples

Below are listed a few Data Exchange scenarios that require Data Standardization:

- Consumer Package Goods brands sell their products through a retail channel. In support of that, brand exchange product sales and inventory data with the retailers. These exchanges involve standardization of inconsistencies in data formats, schemas, and values.
- Travel and hospitality aggregators receive property descriptions and availability data from their airline, car rental, and hotel chain partners. Each data provider may have its own data schema and structure that must be standardized before it can be used.

Holding companies with independent subsidiaries, franchisees, business units, global offices, and external partners receive inconsistent financial data that again must be standardized before it's used. use Lore IO to map and standardize subsidiary sales and finance information to the corporate's model

Handling categorical data

Categorical Data is the data that generally takes a limited number of possible values. Also, the data in the category need not be numerical, it can be textual in nature. All machine learning models are some kind of mathematical model that need numbers to work with. This is one of the primary reasons we need to pre-process the categorical data before we can feed it to machine learning models.

There are two different types of categorical variables:

1. Nominal:

A nominal variable has no intrinsic ordering to its categories. For example, gender is a categorical variable having two categories (Male and Female) with no inherent ordering between them. Another example is Country (India, Australia, America, and so forth).

1. Ordinal:

An ordinal variable has a clear ordering within its categories. For example, consider temperature as a variable with three distinct (but related) categories (low, medium, high). Another example is an education degree (Ph.D., Master's, or Bachelor's).

Different Approaches to Handle Categorical Data

One Hot Encoding

This technique is applied for nominal categorical features. In one Hot Encoding method, each category value is converted into a new column and assigned a value as 1 or 0 to the column.

This will be done using the pandas get_dummies() function and then we will drop the first column in order to avoid dummy variable trap.

Item_Category

Fitness

Food

Kitchen

is converted to

Fitness Food Kitchen

1 0 0

0 1 0

0 0 1

Dummy Encoding

Dummy coding scheme is similar to one-hot encoding. This categorical data encoding method transforms the categorical variable into a set of binary variables (also known as dummy variables). In the case of one-hot encoding, for N categories in a variable, it uses N binary variables. The dummy encoding is a small improvement over one-hot-encoding. Dummy encoding uses N-1 features to represent N labels/categories.

To understand this better let's see the image below. Here we are coding the same data using both one-hot encoding and dummy encoding techniques. While one-hot uses 3 variables to represent the data whereas dummy encoding uses 2 variables to code 3 categories

Column	Code
A	100
B	010
C	001

One- Hot Coding

Column	Code
A	10
B	01
C	00

Dummy Code

Effect Encoding:

This encoding technique is also known as Deviation Encoding or Sum Encoding. Effect encoding is almost similar to dummy encoding, with a little difference. In dummy coding, we use 0 and 1 to represent the data but in effect encoding, we use three values i.e. 1,0, and -1.

The row containing only 0s in dummy encoding is encoded as -1 in effect encoding. In the dummy encoding example, the city Bangalore at index 4 was encoded as 0000. Whereas in effect encoding it is represented by -1-1-1-1.

Hash Encoder

To understand Hash encoding it is necessary to know about hashing. Hashing is the transformation of arbitrary size input in the form of a fixed-size value. We use hashing algorithms to perform hashing operations i.e to generate the hash value of an input. Further, hashing is a one-way process, in other words, one can not generate original input from the hash representation.

Hashing has several applications like data retrieval, checking data corruption, and in data encryption also. We have multiple hash functions available for example Message Digest (MD, MD2, MD5), Secure Hash Function (SHA0, SHA1, SHA2), and many more. By default, the Hashing encoder uses the md5 hashing algorithm but a user can pass any algorithm of his choice.

Binary Encoding

Binary encoding is a combination of Hash encoding and one-hot encoding. In this encoding scheme, the categorical feature is first converted into numerical using an ordinal encoder. Then the numbers are transformed in the binary number. After that binary value is split into different columns.

Binary encoding works really well when there are a high number of categories. For example the cities in a country where a company supplies its products.

	City
0	Delhi
1	Mumbai
2	Hyderabad
3	Chennai
4	Bangalore
5	Delhi
6	Hyderabad
7	Mumbai
8	Agra

	City_0	City_1	City_2	City_3
0	0	0	0	1
1	0	0	1	0
2	0	0	1	1
3	0	1	0	0
4	0	1	0	1
5	0	0	0	1
6	0	0	1	1
7	0	0	1	0
8	0	1	1	0

Base N Encoding

Before diving into BaseN encoding let's first try to understand what is Base here?

In the numeral system, the Base or the radix is the number of digits or a combination of digits and letters used to represent the numbers. The most common base we use in our life is 10 or decimal system as here we use 10 unique digits i.e 0 to 9 to represent all the numbers. Another widely used system is binary i.e. the base is 2. It uses 0 and 1 i.e 2 digits to express all the numbers.

For Binary encoding, the Base is 2 which means it converts the numerical values of a category into its respective Binary form. If you want to change the Base of encoding scheme you may use Base N encoder. In the case when categories are more and binary encoding is not able to handle the dimensionality then we can use a larger base such as 4 or 8.

	City		City_0	City_1	City_2
0	Delhi	**0**	0	0	1
1	Mumbai	**1**	0	0	2
2	Hyderabad	**2**	0	0	3
3	Chennai	**3**	0	0	4
4	Bangalore	**4**	0	1	0
5	Delhi	**5**	0	0	1
6	Hyderabad	**6**	0	0	3
7	Mumbai	**7**	0	0	2
8	Agra	**8**	0	1	1

In the above example, I have used base 5 also known as the Quinary system. It is similar to the example of Binary encoding. While Binary encoding represents the same data by 4 new features the BaseN encoding uses only 3 new variables.

Statistical analysis methods

Descriptive Analysis

Descriptive statistical analysis involves collecting, interpreting, analyzing, and summarizing data to present them in the form of charts, graphs, and tables. Rather than drawing conclusions, it simply makes the complex data easy to read and understand.

Inferential Analysis

The inferential statistical analysis focuses on drawing meaningful conclusions on the basis of the data analyzed. It studies the relationship between different variables or makes predictions for the whole population.

Predictive Analysis

Predictive statistical analysis is a type of statistical analysis that analyzes data to derive past trends and predict future events on the basis of them. It uses machine learning algorithms, data mining, data modelling, and artificial intelligence to conduct the statistical analysis of data.

Prescriptive Analysis

The prescriptive analysis conducts the analysis of data and prescribes the best course of action based on the results. It is a type of statistical analysis that helps you make an informed decision.

Exploratory Data Analysis

Exploratory analysis is similar to inferential analysis, but the difference is that it involves exploring the unknown data associations. It analyzes the potential relationships within the data.

Causal Analysis

The causal statistical analysis focuses on determining the cause and effect relationship between different variables within the raw data. In simple words, it determines why something happens and its effect on other variables. This methodology can be used by businesses to determine the reason for failure.

Graphical analysis methods

Line Plot

The simplest technique, a line plot is used to plot the relationship or dependence of one variable on another. To plot the relationship between the two variables, we can simply call the plot function.

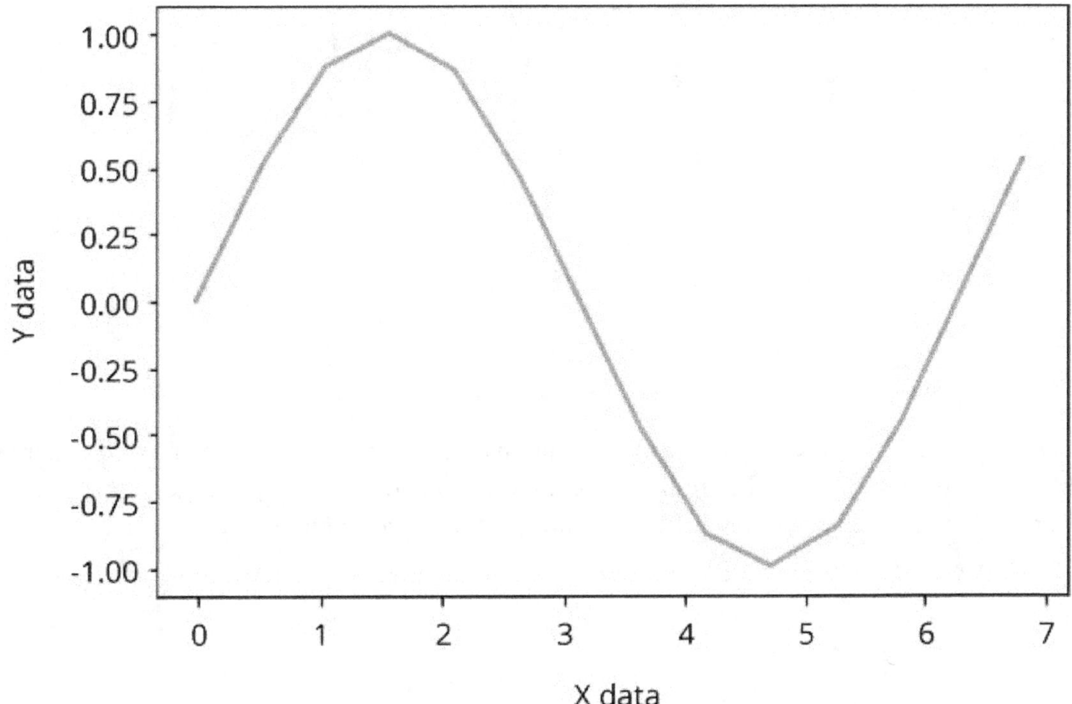

Bar Chart

Bar charts are used for comparing the quantities of different categories or groups. Values of a category are represented with the help of bars and they can be configured with vertical or horizontal bars, with the length or height of each bar representing the value.

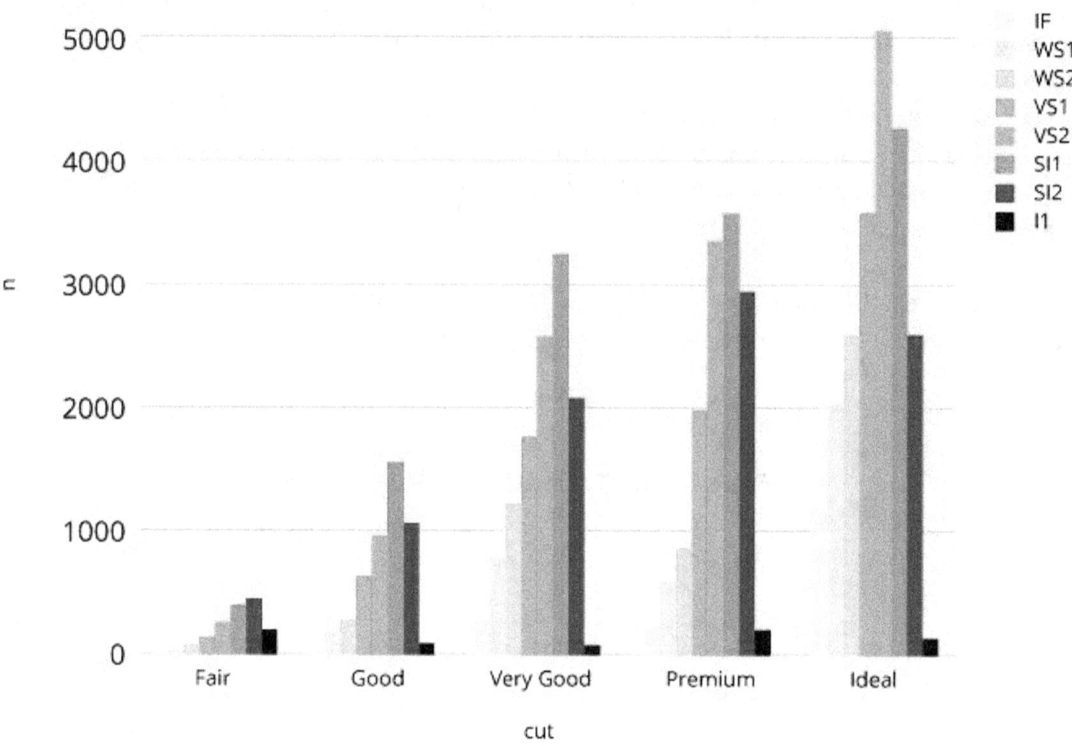

Pie and Donut Charts

There is much debate around the value of pie and donut charts. As a rule, they are used to compare the parts of a whole and are most effective when there are limited components and when text and percentages are included to describe the content. However, they can be difficult to interpret because the human eye has a hard time estimating areas and comparing visual angles.

Donut plot

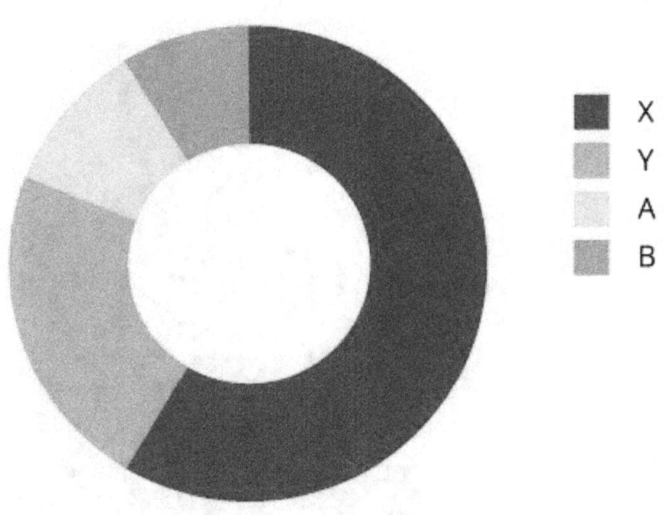

Histogram Plot

A histogram, representing the distribution of a continuous variable over a given interval or period of time, is one of the most frequently used data visualization techniques in machine learning. It plots the data by chunking it into intervals called 'bins'. It is used to inspect the underlying frequency distribution, outliers, skewness, and so on.

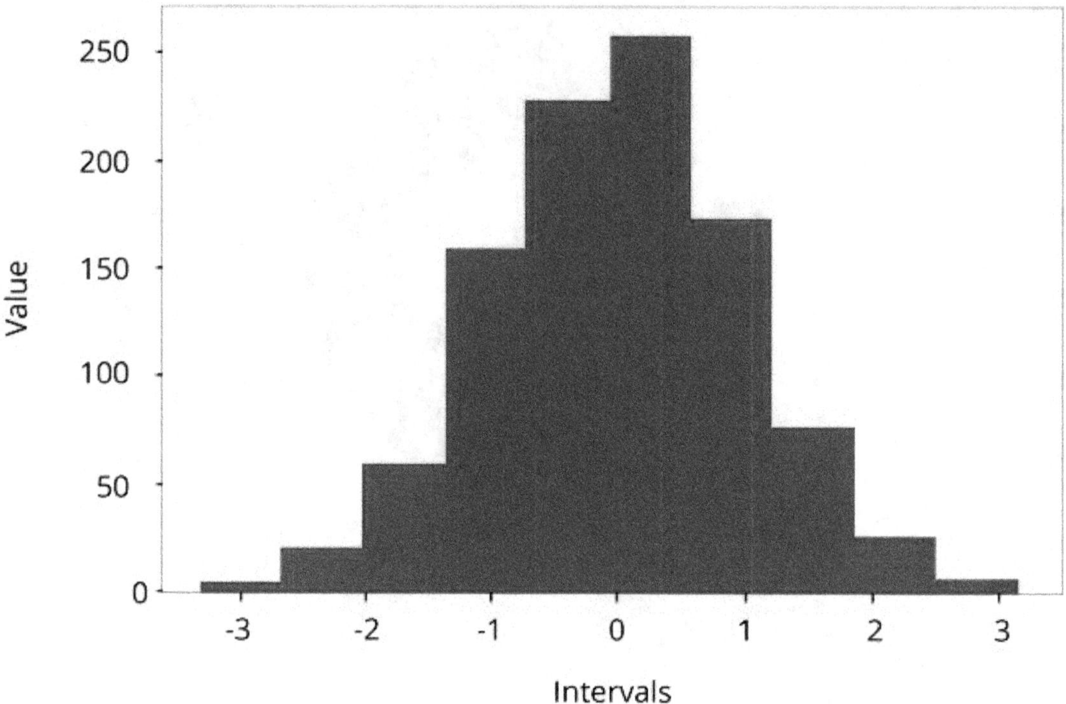

Scatter Plot

Another common visualization techniques is a scatter plot that is a two-dimensional plot representing the joint variation of two data items. Each marker (symbols such as dots, squares and plus signs) represents an observation. The marker position indicates the value for each observation. When you assign more than two measures, a scatter plot matrix is produced that is a series of scatter plots displaying every possible pairing of the measures that are assigned to the visualization. Scatter plots are used for examining the relationship, or correlations, between X and Y variables.

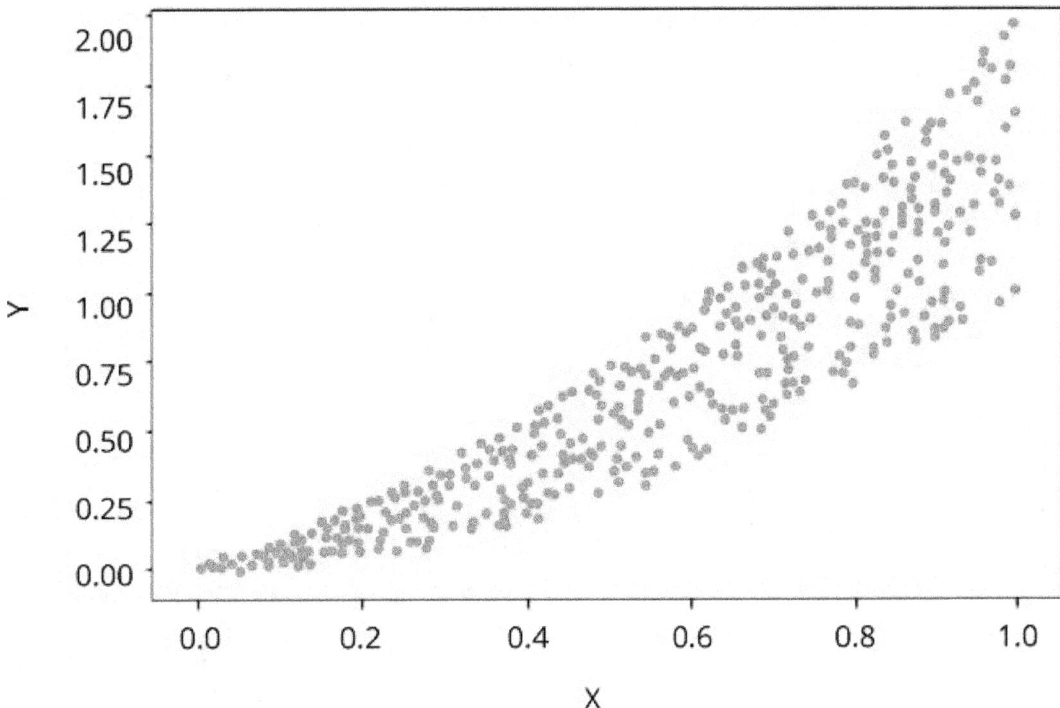

Box and Whisker Plot for Large Data

A binned box plot with whiskers shows the distribution of large data and easily see outliers. In its essence, it is a graphical display of five statistics (the minimum, lower quartile, median, upper quartile and maximum) that summarizes the distribution of a set of data. The lower quartile (25th percentile) is represented by the lower edge of the box, and the upper quartile (75th percentile) is represented by the upper edge of the box. The median (50th percentile) is represented by a central line that divides the box into sections. Extreme values are represented by whiskers that extend out from the edges of the box. Box plots are often used to understand the outliers in the data.

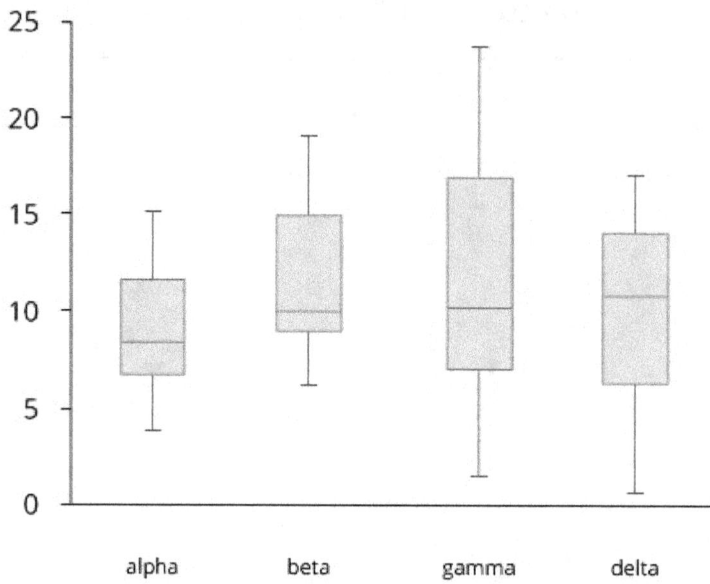

HIVE data Analytics

Hive is a data warehouse system which is used to analyze structured data. It is built on the top of Hadoop. It was developed by Facebook.

Hive provides the functionality of reading, writing, and managing large datasets residing in distributed storage. It runs SQL like queries called HQL (Hive query language) which gets internally converted to MapReduce jobs.

Using Hive, we can skip the requirement of the traditional approach of writing complex MapReduce programs. Hive supports Data Definition Language (DDL), Data Manipulation Language (DML), and User Defined Functions (UDF).

Features of Hive

- Hive is fast and scalable.
- It provides SQL-like queries (i.e., HQL) that are implicitly transformed to MapReduce or Spark jobs.
- It is capable of analyzing large datasets stored in HDFS.
- It allows different storage types such as plain text, RCFile, and HBase.
- It uses indexing to accelerate queries.
- It can operate on compressed data stored in the Hadoop ecosystem.
- It supports user-defined functions (UDFs) where user can provide its functionality.

Limitations of Hive

- Hive is not capable of handling real-time data.
- It is not designed for online transaction processing.
- Hive queries contain high latency.

Hive Architecture

The following architecture explains the flow of submission of query into Hive.

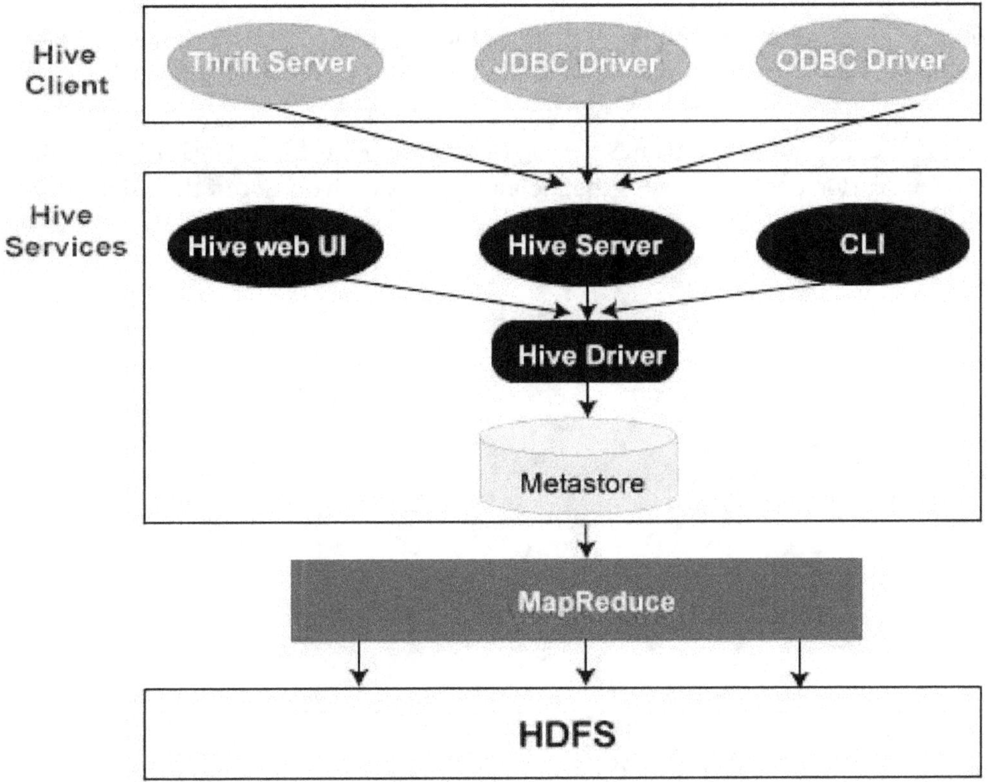

Fig. Hive Architecture

Hive Client

Hive allows writing applications in various languages, including Java, Python, and C++. It supports different types of clients such as:-

- Thrift Server - It is a cross-language service provider platform that serves the request from all those programming languages that supports Thrift.
- JDBC Driver - It is used to establish a connection between hive and Java applications. The JDBC Driver is present in the class org.apache.hadoop.hive.jdbc.HiveDriver.
- ODBC Driver - It allows the applications that support the ODBC protocol to connect to Hive.

Hive Services

The following are the services provided by Hive:-

- Hive CLI - The Hive CLI (Command Line Interface) is a shell where we can execute Hive queries and commands.
- Hive Web User Interface - The Hive Web UI is just an alternative of Hive CLI. It provides a web-based GUI for executing Hive queries and commands.
- Hive MetaStore - It is a central repository that stores all the structure information of various tables and partitions in the warehouse. It also includes metadata of column and its type information, the serializers and deserializers which is used to read and write data and the corresponding HDFS files where the data is stored.

- Hive Server - It is referred to as Apache Thrift Server. It accepts the request from different clients and provides it to Hive Driver.
- Hive Driver - It receives queries from different sources like web UI, CLI, Thrift, and JDBC/ODBC driver. It transfers the queries to the compiler.
- Hive Compiler - The purpose of the compiler is to parse the query and perform semantic analysis on the different query blocks and expressions. It converts HiveQL statements into MapReduce jobs.

Hive Execution Engine - Optimizer generates the logical plan in the form of DAG of map-reduce tasks and HDFS tasks. In the end, the execution engine executes the incoming tasks in the order of their dependencies.